COUNTERING ONLINE HATE SPEECH

Iginio Gagliardone • Danit Gal • Thiago Alves • Gabriela Martinez

Published in 2015 by the United Nations Educational, Scientific and Cultural Organization
7, place de Fontenoy, 75352 Paris 07 SP, France

© UNESCO 2015

ISBN 978-92-3-100105-5

The designations employed and the presentation of material throughout this publication do not imply the expression of
any opinion whatsoever on the part of UNESCO concerning the legal status of any country, territory, city or area or of its
authorities, or concerning the delimitation of its frontiers or boundaries.

The ideas and opinions expressed in this publication are those of the authors; they are not necessarily those of UNESCO
and do not commit the Organization.

This publication was made possible under a contribution by Sweden.

Typeset and printed by UNESCO

Printed in France

Table of Contents

FOREWORD

The opportunities afforded by the Internet greatly overshadow the challenges. While not forgetting this, we can nevertheless still address some of the problems that arise. Hate speech online is one such problem. But what exactly is hate speech online, and how can we deal with it effectively?

As with freedom of expression, on- or offline, UNESCO defends the position that the free flow of information should always be the norm. Counter-speech is generally preferable to suppression of speech. And any response that limits speech needs to be very carefully weighed to ensure that this remains wholly exceptional, and that legitimate robust debate is not curtailed.

In the case of expression of hatred, international standards can help us at a broad level to identify what is hate speech and how we can respond to it:

- For race-related speech, the International Convention on the Elimination of all forms of Racial Discrimination calls for a ban on expressing ideas of superiority or inferiority of people categorised by "race".

- For hatred on the basis of nationality or religion, this is criminalised in terms of Article 20 of the International Covenant on Civil and Political Rights (ICCPR) – but with the qualification that the expressions involved should amount to (i) advocacy, which (ii) constitutes incitement to (iii) discrimination, hostility or violence.

- It is possible, but not required, that hatred such as that based on people's gender, sexual orientation or other features, may be limited in terms of the ICCPR (Article 19), in the interests of respect of the rights or reputations of others.

But in all three cases, any limitations need to be specified in law, rather than arbitrary. They should also meet the criterion of being "necessary" – which requires the limitation to be proportionate and targeted in order to avoid any collateral restriction of legitimate expression which would not be justifiable.

International standards also require that any limitation of expression also has to conform to a legitimate purpose, and cannot just be an exercise of power. Besides for the objective of upholding the rights of others noted above, these purposes can also be national security, public morality or public health.

This complexity calls for an informed and nuanced approach to identifying and limiting "hate speech". Nothing less can ensure an appropriate balance with the free flow of ideas and information. This is especially the case with regard to the world of online expression, as this publication explains.

While the Internet is not separate from the realm of laws, there are complications in developing and applying legal responses to perceived online hate speech. It is for this reason that this study examines social responses which may be considered as complementary to any legal limitations enforced by a state.

A typology of responses is elaborated in this study. One is monitoring and analysis by civil society. A second is individuals promoting peer-to-peer counter-speech. A third is organised action by NGOs to report cases to the authorities, and a fourth is campaigning for actions by Internet companies hosting the particular content. A fifth response is structural – empowering users through education and training about the knowledge, ethics and skills to use the right to freedom of expression on the Internet. This is what UNESCO calls Media and Information Literacy.

It is creative societal responses like these which can produce results. They can help ensure that the Internet remains a place of positive potential, and that this network of networks will help us to build Knowledge Societies on the basis of peace, human rights and sustainable development.

Getachew Engida
Deputy Director-General of UNESCO

1. EXECUTIVE SUMMARY

Hate speech online is situated at the intersection of multiple tensions: it is the expression of conflicts between different groups within and across societies; it is a vivid example of how technologies with a transformative potential such as the Internet bring with them both opportunities and challenges; and it implies complex balancing between fundamental rights and principles, including freedom of expression and the defence of human dignity.

As the UN agency with a specific mandate to foster freedom of expression, and its corollaries, press freedom and freedom of information, UNESCO is actively working to promote mutual knowledge and understanding of peoples, through all means of mass communication, including the Internet in general, and social networking platforms in particular.

The roots of the research presented in this current publication lie in UNESCO's fulfilment of Resolution 52 of its 37th General Conference in November 2013, as agreed by the Organization's 195 Member States. This resolution called for a comprehensive and consultative multistakeholder study, within the mandate of UNESCO, on Internet-related issues of access to information and knowledge, freedom of expression, privacy, and the ethical dimensions of the Information Society. The research into hate speech served as a contribution towards the wider study.[1]

The present report provides a global overview of the dynamics characterizing hate speech online and some of the measures that have been adopted to counteract and mitigate it, highlighting good practices that have emerged at the local and global levels. While the study offers a comprehensive analysis of the international, regional and national normative frameworks developed to address hate speech online, and their repercussions for freedom of expression, it places particular emphasis on social and non-regulatory mechanisms that can help to counter the production, dissemination and impact of hateful messages online.

The findings of this study can be grouped around four main tensions: definition, jurisdiction, comprehension, and intervention.

- **Definition**. Hate speech is a broad and contested term. Multilateral treaties such as the International Covenant on Civil and Political Rights (ICCPR) have sought to define its contours. Multi-stakeholders processes (e.g. the Rabat Plan of Action) have been initiated to bring greater clarity and suggest mechanisms to identify hateful messages. And yet, hate speech continues largely to be used in everyday discourse as a generic term, mixing concrete threats to individuals' and groups' security with cases in which people may be simply venting their anger against authority. Internet intermediaries – organizations that mediate online communication such as Facebook, Twitter, and Google – have advanced their own definitions of hate speech that bind users to a set of rules and allow companies to limit certain forms of expression. National and regional bodies have sought to promote understandings of the term that are more rooted in local traditions. Against this backdrop, the possibility of reaching a universally shared definition seems unlikely, a shared interest to avoid violence and protect human dignity has made debates on hate speech a moment for different stakeholders to come together in original ways and seek locally relevant solutions.

- **Jurisdiction**. The Internet's speed and reach makes it difficult for governments to enforce national legislation in the virtual world. Issues around hate speech online bring into clear relief the emergence of private spaces for expression that serve a public function (e.g. Facebook, Twitter), and the challenges that these spaces pose for regulators. Despite initial resistance, and following public pressure, some of the companies owning these spaces have become more responsive towards tackling the problem of hate speech online, although they have not (yet) been fully incorporated into global debates (e.g. the Rabat Plan of Action) about how to identify and respond to hate speech.

- **Comprehension**. The character of hate speech online and its relation to offline speech and action are poorly understood. These topics are widely talked about – by politicians, activists and academics – but the debates tend to be removed from systematic empirical evidence. The character of perceived hate speech and its possible consequences has led to placing much emphasis on the solutions to the problem and on how they should be grounded in international human rights norms. Yet this very focus has also limited deeper attempts to understand the causes underlying the phenomenon and the dynamics through which certain types of content emerge, diffuse and lead – or not – to actual discrimination, hostility or violence. This study offers various examples of research aimed at mapping the emergence and diffusion of speech online, but also highlights the lack of studies examining the links between hate speech online and other social phenomena, ranging from access to education to rising inequalities.

● **Intervention.** This study identifies a variety of methods that have been used to address specific and contextual problems. Important broader lessons emerge. First, the breadth of the term and the severity of potential harm represent an opportunity for dialogue about definitions, monitoring and contextualisation. Second, the report examines how private companies seek to address instances of hate speech online by favouring user flagging, reporting, and counter-speaking, and how the architectures characterizing different social networking platforms may influence both the diffusion of and the responses to hate speech online. Third, this study shows that dedicated and specialised organizations are extremely important in coalescing individual responses, as well as in putting pressure on companies and public authorities to act. More importantly, different initiatives can complement each other. For example, Internet intermediaries have become increasingly responsive towards requests coming from individual users. However, because they have avoided publishing aggregate results that could offer a broader understanding of the phenomenon, civil society groups have sought to fill this gap, offering global reporting platforms that can collect users' reports. Meanwhile, educational initiatives have been launched to empower individuals so that they would more easily know what and how to report when they encounter cases of hate speech. As the study suggests, there are peculiar elements to the issue of hate speech online that are likely to make it ineffective to focus on actions in isolation or carried out by only one actor. Concerted efforts are needed to adequately tackle this emerging phenomenon.

2. INTRODUCTION

Hate speech lies in a complex nexus with freedom of expression, individual, group and minority rights, as well as concepts of dignity, liberty and equality. Its definition is often contested. In national and international legislation, hate speech refers to expressions that advocate incitement to harm (particularly, discrimination, hostility or violence) based upon the target's being identified with a certain social or demographic group. It may include, but is not limited to, speech that advocates, threatens, or encourages violent acts. For some, however, the concept extends also to expressions that foster a climate of prejudice and intolerance on the assumption that this may fuel targeted discrimination, hostility and violent attacks.

In common parlance, however, definitions of hate speech tend to be broader, sometimes even extending to encompass words that are insulting those in power, or derogatory of individuals who are particularly visible. Especially at critical times, such as during elections, the concept of hate speech may be prone to manipulation: accusations of fomenting hate speech may be traded among political opponents or used by those in power to curb dissent and criticism.

Throughout this study, we will survey different **definitions** of hate speech offered by a variety of actors, from international organizations to social networking platforms, and explain why hate speech is an elusive term. But even if it eschews clear definitions, hate speech (be it conveyed through text, images or sound) can be identified by approximation through the degrading or dehumanizing **functions** that it serves. Drawing on Waldron's work, we can say that an expression that can be considered hateful (be it conveyed through text, images or sound) sends two types of messages. The first is to the targeted group and functions to dehumanize and diminish members assigned to this group. It often sounds more or less like:

> Don't be fooled into thinking you are welcome here. [...] You are not wanted, and you and your families will be shunned, excluded, beaten, and driven out, whenever we can get away with it. We may have to keep a low profile right now. But don't get too comfortable. [...] Be afraid (Waldron 2012).

Another function of hate speech is to let others with similar views know they are not alone, to reinforce a sense of an in-group that is (purportedly) under threat. A typical message sent this time to like-minded individuals can read like:

> We know some of you agree that these people are not wanted here. We know that some of you feel that they are dirty (or dangerous or criminal or terrorist). Know now that you are not alone. [...] There are enough of us around to make sure these people are not welcome. There are enough of us around to draw attention to what these people are really like (Waldron 2012).

Hate speech relies on tensions, which it seeks to re-produce and amplify. Such speech unites and divides at the same time. It creates "us" and "them". For this study, we generally use the term "hate speech" in this wider sense, not restricting the meaning to speech where there is specific incitement of harm.

This study covers a number of axes along which hatred can be constructed, but not necessarily the full range of social categories such as race, ethnicity, language group, gender, religion, sexual preference or nationality. It recognises that, however defined, the notion of hate speech is not about abstract ideas, such as political ideologies, faiths or beliefs – which ideas should not be conflated with specific groups that may subscribe to them. Hate speech concerns antagonism towards people. The study further acknowledges that the biggest problems of hate speech online are currently in countries where there is high Internet connectivity. At the same time, this situation may portend similar developments elsewhere as more people become connected around the world. The study also registers that many of the responses which it assesses have evolved as reactions to cases of online hate speech. In this light, some of these experiences could be considered for adaptation proactively and early-on, rather than only after the emergence of the problem. The purpose of this study is to seek broader lessons from a range of empirical situations.

The hate speech debate

The phenomenon of hate speech calls into question some of the most fundamental principles on which societies are built. The answers each society has developed to balance between freedom of expression and respect for equality and dignity have created unique rifts and alliances at the international level. Much comparative research on hate speech, for example, has focused on the divide that exists between the American and European approaches to regulating hate speech (Rosenfeld 2012; Bleich 2013). The United States has protection of freedom of expression that stretches well beyond the boundaries of speech that is tolerated in Europe. Its emphasis on the clear and present danger that is necessary to be identified in order to ban or punish certain forms of speech has emerged as the defining characteristic of this approach. Numerous European countries, including Germany and France, have adopted instead an approach that not only bans forms of speech because of their likelihood to lead to harm, but also for their intrinsic content.

Other societies have developed unique mechanisms to identify and counter hate speech, which may variously combine customary law and formal law. In Somalia for example, where poetry constitutes a popular vehicle for the dissemination of information and ideas, poets who are seen as repeatedly composing poems which community elders consider to be derogatory of individuals or groups, can be banned from composing new work (Stremlau 2012). Important research has emerged from the study of the role hate speech had in atrocities or major outburst of violence (Kellow and Steeves 1998, Thompson 2007, Yanagizawa-Drott 2010). But systematic research examining the phenomenon of hate speech and its regulation beyond the United States and Europe is still marginal.

Hate speech as a concept has also been contested as too wide-ranging and open to manipulation, and narrower conceptions, including "dangerous speech" and "fear speech", have been advanced to focus on the ability of speech to cause harm and lead to violent outcomes. While hate speech is found – in some form or guise – in almost all societies, including those where the risk of violence is limited, the concept of dangerous speech aims at isolating acts that have a significant probability of "catalysing or amplifying violence by one group against another" (Benesch 2012). Susan Benesch has proposed a framework that can identify a dangerous speech act based on: i) the character and popularity of the speaker; ii) the emotional state of the audience; iii) the content of the speech act itself as a call to action; iv) the historical and social context in which the act occurs; and v) the means used to disseminate it (including the type of language adopted, e.g. if speech is in the vernacular, a person from the area where that language is spoken may hear it differently than if it is in the national language). The concept of "fear speech" (Buyse 2014) has been recently advanced to emphasise language that is able to progressively create a siege mentality and which may ultimately lead to legitimizing violent acts as defensive of a group's safety or integrity. Also based on the study of mass atrocities, the idea of fear speech offers a pathway to understand whether the preconditions for violence may gradually emerge and to possibly identify critical points where counter measures may be most effective.

Finally, there have been some attempts to move beyond simply identifying, regulating and distinguishing countermeasures, and seek instead to understand who the people inciting hatred are and why they do what they do. This type of research, unfortunately, is still marginal, but the Internet and the permanence of textual and visual material it allows are increasing the opportunities for these studies to be carried out. Karmen Erjavec and Melita Poler Kovačič (2012), for example, have analysed hateful messages in the comments on Slovenia's most popular news websites and have been able to interview some of their authors. Their research strategy has led to the identification of different categories of speakers, each motivated by unique factors: from the "soldiers" who belong to political parties and non-governmental organizations and use online means systematically to disseminate stereotypes and damage the reputation of their opponents; to the "watchdogs" who use hate speech to draw attention to social problems. This type of research offers important insights into what motivates certain users to resort to extreme language. As the authors explain, referring to how "soldiers" justify hate speech:

> They claim that online hate speech cannot be compared to hate speech in the traditional media, as this is the only possible means of communication in online comments: "This is the only way of communication; otherwise your voice is simply not heard." Thus, they justify the use of hate speech in comments as "sharp," "military," "the only convincing," and "the only possible" way of communication, which the "enemies" understand (Erjavec & Kovačič 2012, p.910).

Findings like these resonate with research on "internet trolling" (Buckels et al. 2014; Herring et al. 2002; Shin 2008), which is the practice of deliberately provoking users through inflammatory language and upsetting content, and they offer some indications of how the medium can influence the message. More generally, such research seeks a more grounded understanding of the unique characteristics and of some of the causes of a fast evolving phenomenon, rather than simply seeking "solutions" to it.

What distinguishes hate speech online

The proliferation of hate speech **online**, observed by the UN Human Rights Council Special Rapporteur on Minority Issues (HRC, 2015), poses a new set of challenges. While statistics offering a global overview of the phenomenon are not available, both social networking platforms and organizations created to combat hate speech have recognized that hateful messages disseminated online are increasingly common and have elicited unprecedented attention to develop adequate responses.[2] According to **HateBase**, a web-based application that collects instances of hate speech online worldwide, the majority of cases of hate speech target individuals based on ethnicity and nationality, but incitements to hatred focusing on religion and class have also been on the rise.[3]

Hate speech online renders some legal measures elaborated for other media ineffective or inappropriate, and it calls for approaches that are able to take into consideration the specific nature of the interactions enabled by digital information and communication technologies (ICTs). There is the danger of conflating a rant tweeted without thinking of the possible consequences, with an actual threat that is part of a systematic campaign of hatred (Rowbottom 2012). There is the difference between a post that receives little or no attention, and one that goes viral. In addition, there are the complexities that governments and courts may face, for example when trying to enforce a law against a social networking platform headquartered in a different country. Therefore, while hate speech online is not intrinsically different from similar expressions found offline, there are peculiar challenges unique to online content and its regulation. The challenges related to its **endurance**, **itinerancy**, **anonymity** and **transnational** character are among the most complex to address:

The **endurance** of hate speech materials online is a function of its low cost and potential for immediate revival. Hate speech can stay online for a long time in different formats across multiple platforms, which can be linked repeatedly. As Andre Oboler, the CEO of the Online Hate Prevention Institute, has noted, "The longer the content stays available, the more damage it can inflict on the victims and empower the perpetrators. If you remove the content at an early stage you can limit the exposure. This is just like cleaning litter, it doesn't stop people from littering but if you do not take care of the problem it just piles up and further exacerbates."[4] The architecture characterizing different platforms may allow topics to stay alive for shorter or longer periods of time. Twitter's conversations organized around trending topics may facilitate the quick and wide spreading of hateful messages, but they also offer the opportunity for influential speakers to shun messages and possibly end popular threads inciting violence. Facebook, on the contrary, may allow multiple threads to continue in parallel and go unnoticed; creating longer lasting spaces where certain individuals and groups are offended, ridiculed and discriminated.[5]

Hate speech online is also **itinerant**. Even when content is removed, it may find expression elsewhere, possibly on the same platform under a different name or on different online spaces. If a website is shut down, it can quickly reopen using a web-hosting service with less stringent regulations or via the reallocation to a country with laws imposing higher threshold for hate speech. The itinerant nature of hate speech also means that poorly formulated thoughts that would have not found public expression and support in the past may now land on spaces where they can be visible to large audiences.[6] Also in this case, the distinctive architectures characterizing different social networking platforms enable or constrain different forms of expression and responses. From a user's point of view, Facebook sits at the intersection between private and public spheres, where individuals create private online spaces, through which they interact with others online. Even so, a post shared among friends may travel far, reaching unexpected audiences and provoking unintended consequences. Twitter is more clearly designed as a public space offering greater opportunities for a message to be re-broadcast to large audiences and for strangers to respond and engage in public debates. Platforms like Snapchat, in contrast, by deleting conversations among users after they have occurred, offer a greater likelihood that the words will remain within smaller circles.

Anonymity also presents a challenge to dealing with hate speech online. "(T)he internet facilitates anonymous and pseudonymous discourse, which can just as easily accelerate destructive behaviour as it can fuel public discourse" (Citron & Norton 2011). As Drew Boyd, Director of Operations at The Sentinel Project, has stated, "the Internet grants individuals the ability to say horrific things because they think they will not be discovered. This is what makes online hate speech so unique, because people feel much more comfortable speaking hate as opposed to real life when they have to deal with the consequences of what they say".[7] Some governments and social media platforms have sought to enforce real name policies. At the same time, such measures have been deeply contested as they hit at the right to privacy and its intersection with free expression. In addition, the majority of online trolling and hate speech attacks come from pseudonymous accounts, which are not necessarily anonymous to everyone.[8] Genuinely anonymous online communications are rare, as they require the user to employ highly technical measures to ensure that he or she cannot be easily identifiable.

A further complication is the **transnational** reach of the Internet, raising issues of cross-jurisdictional co-operation in regard to legal mechanisms for combatting hate speech. While there are Mutual Legal Assistance treaties in place amongst many countries, these are characteristically slow to work. The transnational reach of many private-sector Internet intermediaries may provide a more effective channel for resolving issues in some cases, although these bodies are also often impacted upon by cross-jurisdictional appeals for data (such as revealing the identity of the author of a particular content). Unlike the dissemination of hate speech through conventional channels, hate speech dissemination online often involves multiple actors, whether knowingly or not. When perpetrators makes use of an online social platform to disseminate their hateful message they do not only hurt their victims, but may also violate terms of service in that platform and at times even state law, depending on their location. The victims, on their part, may feel helpless in the face of online harassment, not knowing to whom they should turn to for help. In the types of responses mapped throughout the study, it appears that collective action, usually undertaken by nongovernmental organizations and lobby groups, has been an effective modus operandi to raise awareness and encourage different stakeholders to take action.

Responses to hate speech online: Legal and non-legal measures

The most debated **responses** to hate speech online have primarily focused on legal definition and legal means, but this approach involves risks and limitations. First, there is the entanglement of law with power. As Robert Post has observed, "Hate speech regulation imagines itself as simply enforcing the given and natural norms of a decent society […]; but from a sociological or anthropological point of view we know that law is always actually enforcing the mores of the dominant group that controls the content of law. For every Machiavelli who urges law to prohibit speech that induces hatred of the state, there is a Walt Whitman who urges us to 'hate tyrants'" (Post et al. 2009). One may note, for example, that hate speech law in Apartheid South Africa was used to criminalise criticism of white domination, which illustrates the potential political abuse of hate speech limitations.[10]

Second, a purely legal lens can miss out on how societies evolve through contestation and disagreement. Although hate speech is an offensive and low expression of dissent, it can also be thought of as a window into deeply-rooted tensions and inequalities, which themselves do need addressing beyond pure speech issues, and beyond the online dimension.

Third, as the UN Human Rights Council Special Rapporteur on Minority Issues states, it is the case that hate crimes rarely occur without prior stigmatization and dehumanization of targeted groups and incitement to hate incidents. At the same time, "only the most egregious forms of hates speech, namely those constituting incitement to discrimination, hostility and violence, are generally considered unlawful." (HRC, 2015). The Rapporteur goes on to note the importance of differentiating between three types of expression (a) expression constituting an offence under international law that can be prosecuted criminally; (b) expression not criminally punishable but that may justify a restriction and a civil suite; (c) expression that does not give rise to criminal or civil sanctions but still raises concerns in terms of tolerance, civility and respect for others. What this highlights is that while there is a role for law in regard to type (a), legal measures cannot be seen as a sufficient response to the full spectrum of speech that can contribute to a climate for hate crimes.

It is in this light that while this study offers a broad overview of the most important legal instruments that regulate hate speech, it places particular emphasis on civil society and social steps rather than state-initiated legal measures. An example of such steps is where, for example, an online community has mobilised to counter and marginalize hateful messages. As stated by the UN Human Rights Council Special Rapporteur on Minority Issues, "while much attention is rightly paid to legal responses to hate speech, equal attention and discussion should be dedicated to non-legal and social responses." (HRC, 2015).

The study's structure is as follows. After a brief discussion of the methodology in Chapter 3, the major debates on hate speech are reviewed in Chapter 4, mapping how international and regional institutions have responded, and reflecting on the new role that companies are playing in regulating expression online. We explain, for example, how international organizations have engaged in consultative processes aimed at giving greater clarity to defining and responding to hate speech. We highlight how a tendency to target governments as the main bearers of duties and responsibilities in public life risks downplaying how new private spaces are also serving a public function, often shaping what and how people communicate. Users of social networks like Facebook or Twitter are subject not only to national law, but also to the social network's terms of service agreements, and to the mechanisms that social networks put in place to enforce them.

Chapter 5 examines the wider significance of four types of initiatives that have been launched to counteract the emergence and/or the spreading of hateful messages: i) research efforts to monitor how hate speech online emerges and spreads, developing early warning systems and methods to distinguish among different typologies of speech acts; ii) coordinated actions by members of the civil society seeking to create national and international coalitions to address emergent threats connecting online hatred and violence offline; iii) initiatives to encourage social networking platforms and Internet Service Providers to play a more robust role in actively responding to hate speech online; and iv) media literacy campaigns and initiatives aimed at preparing users to interpret and react to hateful messages. Building on these cases and on the analysis of ongoing debates regarding the nature of and possible responses to hate speech online, we conclude the study on Chapter 6 with a set of recommendations that can be adopted by a variety of stakeholders to develop practical and tailored responses.

3. METHODOLOGY

This report foregrounds issues of online hate speech and social responses to this phenomenon. Empirical references serve as background to this broader task. The result is an approximate typology of types of social responses that have broad relevance, even though in practice there may often be overlaps between the categories.

The research strategy of this report combined multiple techniques for data collection and analysis. The research began with an extensive literature review covering the traditions that have approached hate speech online from complementary perspectives, including the legal literature that examines how hate speech is addressed in different countries and continents, and the ethnographic studies examining user behaviour in hate-based online spaces. Given the novelty of the phenomenon under investigation and its fast evolving nature, the literature review also included non-academic articles published by experts on their blogs and in specialist publications and major online newspapers and magazines. This first step served the purpose of understanding the contours of the debate and identifying the most pressing questions advanced by different stakeholders from civil society organizations to governments, and private sector companies.

The core of the report builds on an analysis of instances addressing different facets of hate speech online, and it highlights strategies that have emerged to respond, such as by means of organized online actions often promoted by concerned citizens and civil society organizations. Semi-structured interviews were carried out with relevant stakeholders, from representatives of social media platforms, including Facebook and Google, to members of civil society organizations, politicians and technical experts. We also analysed content produced by non-governmental organizations (NGOs) which have launched media and literacy initiatives to counter hate speech online, and the terms of service agreements of online media platforms, including Facebook, Twitter, and YouTube. The aim was to understand the actual monitoring and management of online content. For the issues of hate speech and elections, media and information literacy and coordinated efforts by NGOs, comparisons were also carried out, investigating how monitoring techniques are adapted across countries; how media and information literacy campaigns target different audiences and with what results; and the strategies adopted by anti-discrimination groups or coalitions to lobby social media organizations.

While the range of views and responses to hate speech online is wide, common questions were asked for each of them. The data collection process aimed to understand the delicate balance between monitoring and regulating speech, and fundamental rights, including freedom of expression. In view of the complexities that the Internet has brought to both forms of expression and their regulation, special care was taken to underline that the online sphere was not treated as a separate social space.

4. FRAMEWORKS

Hate speech touches on contested issues of dignity, free expression, liberty and democracy. This chapter outlines key conceptual issues focussing on the tension between hate speech and freedom of expression. It examines how the main international and regional legal instruments address this tension, and how the owners of new private spaces for expression seek to regulate what they variously see as hate speech. It is these diverse frameworks that often form a context and serve as points of reference for social responses to emerge and operate.

Hate speech: examining international principles to identify and counter it

Hate speech is not explicitly mentioned in many international human rights documents and treaties, but it is indirectly called upon by some of the principles related to human dignity and freedom of expression. For example, the 1948 Universal Declaration of Human Rights (UDHR), which was drafted as a response to the atrocities of the World War II, contains the right to equal protection under the law in Article 7, which proclaims that: "All are entitled to equal protection against any discrimination in violation of this Declaration and against any incitement to such discrimination".[11] The UDHR also states that everyone has the right to freedom of expression, which includes "freedom to hold opinions without interference and to seek, receive and impart information and ideas through any media and regardless of frontiers".[12] Taking these Articles together, it can be inferred that everyone has the right to freedom of expression and the right to be protected against discrimination. In other words, everyone has the right to be protected against hate speech insofar as such speech incorporates discriminatory objectives (Morsink 1999).

The UDHR was decisive in setting a framework and agenda for human rights protection, but the Declaration is non-binding. A series of binding documents have been subsequently created to offer a more robust protection for freedom of expression and protection against discrimination. Out of those documents, the International Covenant on Civil and Political Rights (ICCPR) is the most important and comprehensive when addressing hate speech and contains the right to freedom of expression in Article 19 and the prohibition of advocacy to hatred that constitutes incitement to discrimination, hostility or violence in Article 20. Other more tailored international legal instruments contain provisions that have repercussions for the definition of hate speech and identification of responses to it, such as: the Convention on the Prevention and Punishment of the Crime of Genocide (1951), the International Convention on the Elimination of All Forms of Racial Discrimination – ICERD (1969), and, although to a lesser extent, the Convention on the Elimination of All Forms of Discrimination against Women – CEDAW (1981).

Hate Speech and the ICCPR

The ICCPR is the legal instrument most commonly referred to in debates on hate speech and its regulation, although it does not explicitly use the term "hate speech". Article 19, which is often referred to as part of the "core of the Covenant" (Nowak 1993), provides for the right to freedom of expression. This sets out the right, and it also includes general strictures to which any limitation of the right must conform in order to be legitimate.

However, Article 19 is followed by Article 20 that expressly limits freedom of expression in cases of "advocacy of national, racial or religious hatred that constitutes incitement to discrimination, hostility or violence" (Leo et al. 2011). The decision to include this provision, which can be characterised as embodying a particular conceptualisation of hate speech, has been deeply contested. Annotations to the 1955 draft expose divergent opinions.[13] While some countries considered the more generic limitation clause on the right to freedom of expression (in Article 19 paragraph 3) to be sufficient to deal with hate speech, others campaigned in favour of a stand-alone provision (Article 20) which expressly prohibits hatred that constitutes incitement to harm (Nowak 1993). Even when the final document came to the ratification stage, some signatories of the ICCPR placed reservations on Article 20.[14] This is a common practice, as many countries place reservations when they sign international treaties, yet it underscores the tensions related to Article 20 and its contrast with Article 19. The Human Rights Committee, the UN body created by the ICCPR to oversee its implementation, cognizant of the tension, has sought to stress that Article 20 is fully compatible with the right to freedom of expression.[15]

To elaborate on these points, and their application to online expression, the ICCPR can be examined in more detail. Article 19 (2) of the ICCPR states that "(e)veryone shall have the right to freedom of expression; this right shall include freedom to seek, receive and impart information and ideas of all kinds, regardless of frontiers, either orally, in writing or in print, in the form of art, or through any other media of his choice".[16] The expression 'of all kinds' implies that States cannot exclude unwanted content from the scope of protection of the right to freedom of expression (Nowak 1993).[17] And the reference to "any other media of his choice"[18] allows extending freedom of expression to new forms of technology, including the Internet.[19] To make this point even more explicit, the UN Human Rights Committee in its General Comment 34 specifically refers to the Internet and other mobile technologies and urges States to "take all necessary steps to foster the independence of these new media and to ensure access of individuals thereto".[20]

In the ICCPR, the right to freedom of expression is not an absolute right. It can legitimately be limited by states under restricted circumstances:

> 3. The exercise of the rights provided for in paragraph 2 of this article carries with it special duties and responsibilities. It may therefore be subject to certain restrictions, but these shall only be such as are provided by law and are necessary:

(a) For respect of the rights or reputations of others;

(b) For the protection of national security or of public order (ordre public), or of public health or morals.[21]

Limitations should not impair the essence of the right.[22] As a general principle, limitations to human rights under the Covenant "must constitute an exception to the rule and must be kept to the minimum necessary to pursue the legitimate aim of safeguarding other human rights established in the Covenant".[23] Limitations imposed by states may include online speech under Article 19 (3) of the ICCPR, as the Human Rights Committee explains in General Comment 34:

> Any restrictions on the operation of websites, blogs or any other Internet-based, electronic or other such information dissemination system, including systems to support such communication, such as Internet service providers or search engines, are only permissible to the extent that they are compatible with paragraph 3. Permissible restrictions generally should be content-specific; generic bans on the operation of certain sites and systems are not compatible with paragraph 3. It is also inconsistent with paragraph 3 to prohibit a site or an information dissemination system from publishing material solely on the basis that it may be critical of the government or the political social system espoused by the government.[24]

Between Article 19 (3) and Article 20, there is a distinction between optional and obligatory limitations to the right to freedom of expression. Article 19 (3) states that limitations on freedom of expression "**may** therefore be subject to certain restrictions", as long as they are provided by law and necessary to certain legitimate purposes. Article 20 states that any advocacy of (certain kinds of) hatred that constitutes incitement to discrimination, hostility or violence "**shall be** prohibited by law".

Despite indications on the gravity of speech offenses that should be prohibited by law under Article 20, there remains complexity.[25] In particular there is a grey area in conceptualising clear distinctions between (i) expressions of hatred, (ii) expression that advocate hatred, and (iii) hateful speech that specifically constitutes incitement to the practical harms of discrimination, hostility or violence. Thus, while states have an obligation to prohibit speech conceived as "advocacy to hatred that constitutes incitement to discrimination, hostility or violence", as consistent with Article 20 (2),[26] how to interpret such is not clearly defined.[27] Consequently, limitations on freedom of expression, based on the ICCPR provision, may be open to abuse,[28] as reported by some NGOs.[29] The Camden Principles, a set of standards formulated by the NGO Article 19 in consultation with human rights experts, define specific criteria to avoid misapplication of Article 20 (2), explaining that: "States should not prohibit criticism directed at, or debate about, particular ideas, beliefs or ideologies, or religions or religious institutions, unless such expression constitutes hate speech".[30] It is important to stress that Article 20 needs to be interpreted narrowly (Eltayeb 2008), to avoid misuse of the concept. As Ghanea explains, "whilst prohibited by law, a well calibrated process of responding to hate speech that incites discrimination needs to be carefully ascertained in order for the sanctions adopted at each stage to indeed be 'appropriate'" (Ghanea 2008).

Given this complexity and risks of abuse of international norms to restrict legitimate speech, the UN has sought to create spaces for promoting a shared understanding of what hate speech is and how it should be addressed, but also for allowing regional, national and local sensitivities to be taken into account. The UN High Commissioner for Human Rights (OHCHR), in particular, organized a series of consultative meetings that led in 2012 to the formulation of the Rabat Plan of Action on the prohibition of "national, racial or religious hatred that constitutes incitement to discrimination, hostility or violence."[31] The Rabat Plan of Action acknowledges that, despite the obligations for states that are ICCPR signatories, many legal frameworks do not contain legal prohibition of such advocacy or that some laws that do so also use terminology that is inconsistent with Article 20 of the ICCPR.[32] It also proposed a six part threshold test to identify hate messages, considering context, speaker, intent, content, extent of the speech and likelihood the speech could incite actual harm.[33] However, as further highlighted later in this chapter and in this study more generally, in the case of *online* hate speech, the emphasis that the Rabat Plan of Action places on national level actors and especially states, may underplay the significance of private sector social networking platforms that operate trans-nationally. These actors can play a highly meaningful role in interpreting hate speech and allowing or constraining expression. In addition, the Rabat Plan also does not give much attention to issues of incitement on grounds such as gender, sexual preference or language.

Other international legal instruments

The International Convention on the Elimination of All Forms of Racial Discrimination (ICERD), which came into force in 1969, has also implications for conceptualising forms of hate speech. The ICERD differs from the ICCPR in three respects.

First, its conceptualisation of hate speech is specifically limited to speech that refers to race and ethnicity.

Second, it asserts in Article 4, paragraph (a), that state parties:

> Shall declare as an offence punishable by law all dissemination of ideas based on racial superiority or hatred, incitement to racial discrimination, as well as all acts of violence or incitement to such acts against any race or group of persons of another colour or ethnic origin, and also the provision of any assistance to racist activities, including the financing thereof;

This obligation imposed by the ICERD on state parties is also stricter than the case of Article 20 of the ICCPR covering the criminalisation of racist ideas that are not necessarily inciting discrimination, hostility or violence.

Third, an important difference is in the issue of intent. The concept of "advocacy of hatred" introduced in the ICCPR is more specific than discriminatory speech described in the ICERD, since it is taken to require consideration of the intent of author and not the expression in isolation – this is because "advocacy" is interpreted in the ICCPR as requiring the intent to sow hatred.[34] The mere dissemination of messages of racial superiority or hatred, or even incitement to racial discrimination or violence, shall be punishable in accordance to the ICERD. But in the ICCPR, the intent to incite hatred needs to be proved, in order for the offence to be prohibited under Article 20 (2).

The Committee on the Elimination of Racial Discrimination has actively addressed hate speech in its General Recommendation 29, in which the Committee recommends state parties to:

> (r) Take measures against any dissemination of ideas of caste superiority and inferiority or which attempt to justify violence, hatred or discrimination against descent-based communities;

> (s) Take strict measures against any incitement to discrimination or violence against the communities, including through the Internet;

> (t) Take measures to raise awareness among media professionals of the nature and incidence of descent-based discrimination;[35]

These points, which reflect the ICERD's reference to the dissemination of expression, have significance for the Internet. The expression of ideas in some online contexts may immediately amount to spreading them. This is especially relevant for private spaces that have begun to play a public role, as in the case of many social networking platforms.

Similarly to the ICERD, the Genocide Convention aims to protect groups defined by race, nationality or ethnicity, although it also extends its provisions to religious groups. When it comes to hate speech, however, the Genocide Convention is limited only to acts that publicly incite to genocide, recognized as "acts committed with intent to destroy, in whole or in part, a national, ethnical, racial or religious group", regardless of whether such acts are undertaken in peacetime or in wartime (Defeis 1992).

Specifically gender-based hate speech (as distinct from discriminatory actions) is not covered in depth in international law. The Convention on the Elimination of All Forms of Discrimination against Women (CEDAW), which entered into force in 1981, imposes obligations on states to condemn discrimination against women[36] and "prevent, investigate, prosecute and punish" acts of gender-based violence.[37] The Human Rights Committee has also expressed "grave concern at acts of violence and discrimination, in all regions of the world, committed against individuals because of their sexual orientation and gender identity."[38] The extent of which expression links to such practical actions is a subject of debate. However, the UN Human Rights Committee in General Comment 28 called for states to "provide information about legal measures to restrict the publication or dissemination" of pornographic material which portrays women as objects of degrading treatment.[39]

This review, though far from comprehensive, shows that international law allows states to take measures to limit hate speech. There is also some provision for individuals to bring complaints about speech to established mechanisms of the protection of human rights by different treaties: the Human Rights Committee receives individual complaints related to the ICCPR, the Committee on the Elimination of Racial Discrimination receives complaints from the ICERD, and in the case of the CEDAW the responsible body for dealing with these complaints is the Committee on the Elimination of Discrimination against Women. However, individuals may only bring a complaint against a state that has explicitly allowed (through ratification of an Optional Protocol) for such mechanisms.

A tabular representation helps to show the range of speech under which particular hateful utterances may fall in terms of selected international standards (adapted from Ghanea 2013):

CATEGORY	Dissemination of ideas of (racial/ ethnic) superiority and hatred	Advocacy of hatred that constitutes incitement to hostility, discrimination or violence	Incitement to terrorism	Incitement to genocide
EXAMPLE	(e.g. see CERD General Recommendation 29)	(e.g. see Article 20 ICCPR)	(e.g. see "Incitement to commit terrorist act or acts" in Article 1 (1) of SC Resolution 1624 (2005))	(e.g. see "direct and public incitement to commit genocide in Article 3(c) of the 1948 Convention of the Prevention and Punishment of the Crime of Genocide)

Regional responses to hate speech

Diverse opinions on balancing freedom of expression and limitations around hate speech find pronounced manifestation in regional human rights instruments. These documents complement international treaties as they reflect regional particularities that are not specified in treaties with universal reach. Regional instruments may be particularly effective to enforce the protection of human rights as in the case of the European Court of Human Rights, which decides more cases related to hate speech than the United Nations Human Rights Committee. Nevertheless, regional human rights instruments ought not to contradict established international norms, nor impose stronger limitations on fundamental rights. Most regional instruments do not have specific articles prescribing prohibition of hate speech, but they more generally allow states to limit freedom of expression – which provisions can be applied to specific cases. This section examines how the right to freedom of expression and its limitations are defined at the regional level and how regional documents complement other texts that allow for definition and limitation of hate speech.

The **American Convention on Human Rights** describes limitations on freedom of expression in a manner similar to the ICCPR in Article 19 (3). The Convention adds a specific limitation clause prohibiting prior censorship; however, in order to offer more protection to children, it allows prior censorship for the "moral protection of childhood and adolescence".[40] The Organization of American States has also adopted another declaration on the principles of freedom of expression, which includes a specific clause stating that "prior conditioning of expressions, such as truthfulness, timeliness or impartiality is incompatible with the right to freedom of expression recognized in international instruments".[41] The Inter-American Court has advised that "(a)buse of freedom of information thus cannot be controlled by preventive measures but only through the subsequent imposition of sanctions on those who are guilty of the abuses".[42] The Court also imposes a test for States willing to enact restrictions on freedom of expression, as they need to observe the following requirements: "a) the existence of previously established grounds for liability; b) the express and precise definition of these grounds by law; c) the legitimacy of the ends sought to be achieved; d) a showing that these grounds of liability are 'necessary to ensure' the aforementioned ends."[43] Finally, the Inter-American System has a Special Rapporteur on Freedom of Expression who conducted a comprehensive study on hate speech. His conclusion was that the Inter-American Human Rights System differs from the UN and the European approach on a key point: The Inter-American system covers only hate speech that actually leads to violence, and solely such speech can be restricted.[44]

The **African Charter on Human Rights and Peoples' Rights** takes a different approach in Article 9 (2), allowing for restrictions on rights as long as they are "within the law". This concept has been criticized and there is a vast amount of legal scholarship on the so-called "claw-back" clauses and their interpretation (Viljoen 2012). The criticism is mainly aimed at the fact that countries can manipulate their own legislation and weaken the essence of the right to freedom of expression. However, it is important to add that the Declaration of Principles on Freedom of Expression in Africa elaborates a higher standard for limitations on freedom of expression. It declares that the right "should not be restricted on public order or national security grounds unless there is a real risk of harm to a legitimate interest and there is a close causal link between the risk of harm and the expression".[45]

In 1990, the Organization of the Islamic Conference (which was later renamed Organization of Islamic Cooperation – OIC) adopted the **Cairo Declaration on Human Rights in Islam** (CDHRI) which, in its preamble, states the principle that human rights should be "in accordance with the Islamic Shari'ah".[46] This clause may be seen to impact on the threshold for limitations. The principle that human rights are subject to the Shari'ah is why OIC member states have called for criminalisation of speech that extends beyond cases of imminent violence to encompass "acts or speech that denote manifest intolerance and hate".[47] The right to freedom of expression in the Article 22 of the CDHRI, is formulated in the following manner:

(a) Everyone shall have the right to express his opinion freely in such manner as would not be contrary to the principles of the Shari'ah.

(b) Everyone shall have the right to advocate what is right, and propagate what is good, and warn against what is wrong and evil according to the norms of Islamic Shari'ah

(c) Information is a vital necessity to society. It may not be exploited or misused in such a way as may violate sanctities and the dignity of Prophets, undermine moral and ethical values or disintegrate, corrupt or harm society or weaken its faith.

(d) It is not permitted to arouse nationalistic or doctrinal hatred or to do anything that may be an incitement to any form of racial discrimination.[48]

The **Arab Charter on Human Rights**, which was adopted by the Council of the League of Arab States in 2004, includes in Article 32 provisions that are relevant also for online communication as it guarantees the right to "freedom of opinion and expression, and the right to seek, receive and impart information and ideas through any medium, regardless of geographical boundaries".[49] It allows a limitation on a broad basis in paragraph 2 "Such rights and freedoms shall be exercised in conformity with the fundamental values of society".[50] This position is different to that of the Human Rights Committee General Comment No. 22, which states that "the concept of morals derives from many social, philosophical and religious traditions; consequently, limitations on the freedom to manifest a religion or belief for the purpose of protecting morals must be based on principles not deriving exclusively from a single tradition".[51]

The **ASEAN Human Rights Declaration** includes the right to freedom of expression in Article 23. Article 7 of the Declaration provides for general limitations, affirming, "the realisation of human rights must be considered in the regional and national context bearing in mind different political, economic, legal, social, cultural, historical and religious backgrounds."[52] In this regard, the Office of the High Commissioner on Human Rights has drawn attention to the Vienna Declaration's provision which asserts that, notwithstanding differences, "it is the duty of states, regardless of their political, economic and cultural systems, to promote and protect all human rights and fundamental freedoms".[53]

This brief discussion indicates that, compared to international standards, some regional texts are potentially more restrictive of freedom of expression. In other regional texts, however, there are even narrower tests than international standards for assessing what limitations of freedom of expression can be considered legitimate.

The Charter of Fundamental Rights of the European Union which declares the right to freedom of expression in Article 11, has a clause which prohibits abuse of rights. It asserts that the Charter must not be interpreted as implying any "limitation to a greater extent than is provided for therein".[54] An example of a limitation which implies a strict test of necessity and proportionality is the provision on freedom of expression in the European Convention on Human Rights, which underlines that the exercise of freedom of expression carries duties and responsibilities. Therefore, it "may be subject to such formalities, conditions, restrictions or penalties as are prescribed by law and are necessary in a democratic society, in the interests of national security, territorial integrity or public safety, for the prevention of disorder or crime, for the protection of health or morals, for the protection of the reputation or rights of others, for preventing the disclosure of information received in confidence, or for maintaining the authority and impartiality of the judiciary".[55] The European Court of Human Rights is careful to distinguish between hate speech and the right of individuals to express their views freely, even if others take offence.[56]

There are regional instances relevant specifically to online hate speech. The Council of Europe (CoE) in 2000 issued a General Policy Recommendation on Combating the Dissemination of Racist, Xenophobic and Anti-Semitic Material via the Internet.[57] The creation of the CoE Convention on Cybercrime in 2001, which regulates mutual assistance regarding investigative powers, provides signatory countries with a mechanism to deal with computer data, which would include trans-national hate speech online.[58] In 2003 the CoE launched an additional protocol to the Convention on Cybercrime which addresses online expression of racism and xenophobia. The convention and its protocol were opened for signature and ratification of countries outside Europe, and other countries, such as Canada and South Africa, are already part of this convention. The Protocol imposes an obligation on Member States to criminalise racist and xenophobic insults online of "(i) persons for the reason that they belong to a group distinguished by race, colour, descent or national or ethnic origin, as well as religion, if used as a pretext for any of these factors; or (ii) a group of persons which is distinguished by any of these characteristics".[59]

Summing up international provisions for limiting speech

Article 19 (3) of the ICCPR gives strict criteria for limitations on freedom of expression, and these may be applied in the cases where regional human rights systems are very broad in their limitations. In the ICCPR, the requirement "provided by law" for instance, means that "restrictions on freedom of expression and information must be set down in formal legislation or an equivalent unwritten norm of common law and adequately specify the permissibility of given interference by enforcement organs" (Nowak 1993). In addition, the issue of purpose is relevant. The ICCPR states that freedom of expression may only be limited "for respect of the rights or reputations of others" or "for the protection of national security or of public order (ordre public), or of public health or morals".[60] As the Human Rights Committee explains in General Comment 34:

> Restrictions are not allowed on grounds not specified in paragraph 3, even if such grounds would justify restrictions to other rights protected in the Covenant. Restrictions must be applied only for those purposes for which they were prescribed and must be directly related to the specific need on which they are predicated.[61]

There is a pattern in international law which emphasises the mutuality between freedom of expression and protection against hate speech. Recent documents such as the Human Rights Committee General Comment 34 and the Rabat Plan of Action have repeatedly done this. The latter gives an overview:

> Under international human rights standards, which are to guide legislation at the national level, expression labelled as "hate speech" can be restricted under articles 18 and 19 of the ICCPR on different grounds, including respect for the rights of others, public order, or even sometimes national security. States are also obliged to "prohibit" expression that amounts to "incitement" to discrimination, hostility or violence (under article 20.2 of the ICCPR and, under some different conditions, also under article 4 of the ICERD).[62]

In overview, balancing freedom of expression and limitations as regards hatred is a highly complex matter in terms of both international laws and regional counterparts. This accounts for the diversity of legal conceptions of hate speech around the world, and complicates further the interpretation of law in any given case. What is clear is that any legal limitations always need to be considered adjacent to the broader right to freedom of expression, and "the relation between right and restriction and between norm and exception must not be reversed".[63]

Private spaces of expression and hate speech

The international and regional legal instruments surveyed so far offer a framework for *states* to address hate speech within their duty to promote and protect rights, which includes balancing rights to freedom of expression with rights to dignity, equality and safety. When dealing with hate speech *online*, however, individual states are not always the most impactful actors. Internet intermediaries such as social networking platforms, Internet Service Providers or Search Engines, stipulate in their terms of service how they may intervene in allowing, restricting, or channelling the creation and access to specific content. A vast amount of online interactions occur on social networking platforms that transcend national jurisdictions and which platforms have also developed their own definitions of hate speech and measures to respond to it. For a user who violates the terms of service, the content he or she has posted may be removed from the platform, or its access may be restricted to be viewed only by a certain category of users (e.g. users living outside a specific country).

The principles that inspire terms of service agreements and the mechanisms that each company develops to ensure their implementation have significant repercussions on the ability that people have to express themselves online as well as to be protected from hate speech.

Most intermediaries have to enter in negotiations with national governments to an extent that varies according to the type of intermediary, areas where the company is registered, and the legal regime that applies. As Tsesis explains, "(i)f transmissions on the Internet are sent and received in particular locations, then specific fora retain jurisdiction to prosecute illegal activities transacted on the Internet" (Tsesis 2001). Internet Service Providers are the most directly affected by national legislation because they have to be located in a specific country to operate. Search Engines, while they can modify search results for self-regulatory or commercial reasons, have increasingly tended to adapt to the intermediary liability regime of both their registered home jurisdictions and other jurisdictions in which they provide their services, either removing links to content proactively or upon request by authorities (MacKinnon et al. 2015).

All Internet intermediaries operated by private companies, however, are also expected to respect human rights. This is set out in the Guiding Principles on Business and Human Rights elaborated by the United Nations Office of the High Commissioner for Human Rights. The document emphasizes corporate responsibility in upholding human rights. In principle 11, it declares that: "Business enterprises should respect human rights. This means that they should avoid infringing on the human rights of others and should address adverse human rights impacts with which they are involved".[64]

To address these issues, Internet intermediaries, in line with other companies, should assess "actual and potential human rights impacts integrating and acting upon the findings, tracking responses, and communicating how impacts are addressed."[65] The UN Guiding Principles also indicate that in cases in which human rights are violated, companies should "provide for or cooperate in their remediation through legitimate processes".[66] In the case of Internet intermediaries and conceptions of hate speech, this means that they should ensure that measures are in place to provide a commensurate response.

These principles, however, are still struggling to find a concrete implementation in everyday practice. One issue is the extent to which a private sector entity has the right to set terms of service which may be more restrictive of speech than what a state is required to permit in terms of international standards such as the ICCPR. This is analogous in some respects to press freedom in which a media outlet is entitled to set its own editorial policy, even though social media is also distinctly based upon the expressions of users rather the situation of news media where expressions emanate from those employed by the platform itself. Another issue is how companies, inasmuch as they follow international human rights standards, decide on the balance of rights, such as freedom of expression in relation to privacy, equality or dignity. Finally, there are issues about how companies make decisions when national laws are not compliant with international human rights standards such as for legitimate limits on freedom of expression.

Natasha Lomas has polemically written in the case of online harassment: "Twitter shrugs its turquoise shoulders at the problem of online harassment, takes a moment to oil its feathers and then chirps that 'the tweets must flow' (unless of course it's legally compelled to act)".[67] In the face of such sentiments, Internet intermediaries, responding in part to this kind of pressure, have shown willingness to reconsider some of their policies and increase their transparency.[68] In general, the situation is dynamic and continues to develop.

How hate speech is defined and regulated in private spaces for expression

Internet intermediaries have developed disparate definitions of hate speech and guidelines to regulate it. Some companies do not use the term hate speech, but have a descriptive list of terms related to it. *Yahoo!*'s terms of service prohibit the posting of "content that is unlawful, harmful, threatening, abusive, harassing, tortuous, defamatory, vulgar, obscene, libellous, invasive of another's privacy, hateful, or racially, ethnically or otherwise objectionable".[69] Similarly, Twitter does not mention explicitly a prohibition of hate speech, but alerts its users that they "may be exposed to Content that might be offensive, harmful, inaccurate or otherwise inappropriate, or in some cases, postings that have been mislabelled or are otherwise deceptive". As its terms of service continue, "Under no circumstances will Twitter be liable in any way for any Content, including, but not limited to, any errors or omissions in any Content, or any loss or damage of any kind incurred as a result of the use of any Content posted, emailed, transmitted or otherwise made available via the Services or broadcast elsewhere."[70] This is complemented by Twitter's Rules, a set of conditions for users that contain content limitations such as "You may not publish or post direct, specific threats of violence against others".[71] As further explained below and in Chapter 5, Twitter has responded to hate speech related requests coming from governments and civil society organizations to act on content.

Other companies make explicit reference to hate speech. *YouTube*'s terms of service, for example, seek to balance freedom of expression and limitations to some forms of content. As they read, "We encourage free speech and defend everyone's right to express unpopular points of view. But we do not permit hate speech: speech which attacks or demeans a group based on race or ethnic origin, religion, disability gender, age, veteran status and sexual orientation/ gender identity."[72] This definition is thus wider than the ICCPR's call for limitation only of speech that constitutes intentional advocacy of hatred that incites discrimination, hostility or violence. It is an example of how private companies can be more restrictive than international law, and even some regional or national laws on hate speech.

Facebook's terms forbid content that is harmful, threatening or which has potential to stir hatred and incite violence. In its community standards, Facebook elaborates that "Facebook removes hate speech, which includes content that directly attacks people based on their: race, ethnicity, national origin, religious affiliation, sexual orientation, sex, gender or gender identity, or serious disabilities or diseases". [73] It further states that "We allow humour, satire or social commentary related to these topics, and we believe that when people use their authentic identity, they are more responsible when they share this kind of commentary. For that reason, we ask that Page owners associate their name and Facebook Profile with any content that is insensitive, even if that content does not violate our policies. As always, we urge people to be conscious of their audience when sharing this type of content".[74]

Microsoft has specific rules concerning hate speech for a variety of its applications. Its policy for mobile phones prohibits applications that "contain any content that advocates discrimination, hatred, or violence based on considerations of race, ethnicity, national origin, language, gender, age, disability, religion, sexual orientation, status as a veteran, or membership in any other social group."[75] The company has also rules regarding online gaming, which prohibit any communication that is indicative of "hate speech, controversial religious topics and sensitive current or historical events".[76] This is another example of how private companies can be more restrictive than regional or international law on hate speech: "Controversial religious topics and sensitive current or historical events" are not necessarily prohibited in international law, nor are they automatically considered discriminatory. Nevertheless, in order to promote what they see as a safer online community, Microsoft has chosen to impose restrictive regulations on certain products that it offers. On the other hand, these terms of service may be more liberal than the legal limits in certain jurisdictions.

Definition and implementation

Typically, only a small minority of users read the terms of service[77] and there are different levels of "quality" among the various types of agreement.[78] The biggest challenge is possibly not so much how Internet intermediaries define hate speech, but how they enforce their definitions. An issue here is the liability of these intermediaries. Many intermediaries argue that they do not generate or control content online, and therefore should only have limited liability.[79] This is interpreted to exempt them from prior screening or moderation of content, and only expose them after publication if their attention is drawn to content that offends law and/or their terms of service. There are different legal regimes worldwide on liability, with different impacts, but ultimately there is likely to be at least one jurisdictional standard which can enforce an intervention by the company to limit a particular instance of online speech.

The notion of limited liability distinguishes Internet intermediaries from news media companies. There are debates, however, over the extent to which news media should also have limited liability for user-generated comments on their websites. Their practices and terms of service for moderating content, as well as their self-regulatory systems such as press councils, may at any rate have significance for Internet intermediaries. A case examining xenophobic hate speech in South Africa concluded by asking whether online interactive news media had a different role as regards any decisions to limit speech, as compared to print and broadcast media.[80]

For Internet Service Providers (ISPs), liability to a given jurisdiction is relatively straightforward. Similarly to other Internet intermediaries they can define their own parameters when offering a service, but, since they are bound by the principle of territoriality, they tend to operate in terms of the laws of the country where they are offering service (Ryngaert 2008). This makes them more responsive than other intermediaries to external requests to remove specific content (Goldsmith & Wu 2006; Kohl 2002).

The issue becomes more complex for social networking platforms with a global reach (e.g. Facebook, Twitter). Given the enormous amount of data they handle, social networking platforms mainly rely on notifications from users who report content they consider inappropriate, offensive, or dangerous. The platforms then decide, mainly according to their terms of service, whether or not this content should be removed or whether other actions need to be taken to restrict access to it or the ability of its authors to continue using the platform's service. In the absence of multiple national jurisdictional authority over the company, and the limited capacity and reach of any single jurisdiction except that in which the operation is domiciled, many intermediaries tend to operate according to their own overarching global terms of service.

Apart from old guidelines leaked by employees of companies to which social networking platforms outsourced some aspects of content regulation,[81] little is known about how terms of service translate in practice about what to keep and what to filter or remove. Some have suggested that Facebook has been developing a set of objective standards to act upon speech which they consider likely to provoke violence.[82] But when interviewed for this study, Monika Bickert, Facebook's Head of Global Policy Management, indicated that Facebook tries to avoid a textbook approach and prefers to look at context as much as possible.[83]

Some companies have become more attentive to users' complaints over time. In 2012 Facebook introduced the possibility for users who flag content which they consider inappropriate to track their reports until the issue is resolved.[84] It has also offered tools to "socialize" reporting, allowing users to privately notify the author of a specific piece of content before formally asking Facebook for it to be removed. These new opportunities represent interesting additions to other measures to respond to perceived hate speech, even if evidence is lacking about how effective they have been over time and whether or not users are satisfied with the options they are being offered.

In another instance, YouTube has reportedly given special status to flag content to some British agencies which seek to remove the Islamic State's (IS) propaganda from the platform.[85] In Malaysia, Google reportedly deleted a blog on its Blogger platform on the grounds that its content crossed "the line by publishing hate speech [...] content that promotes hate or violence towards groups based on race, ethnicity, religion, disability, gender, age, veteran status or sexual orientation/gender identity", terms that the company also applies to YouTube.[86]

In general, as some specific instances analysed in the following chapter indicate, while Internet intermediaries tend to invoke their terms of service when deciding whether or not a specific type of content should be removed, they have also demonstrated certain flexibility in receiving demands from a variety of actors. Twitter, for example, in responding to popular pressure in the aftermath of a case of abuse against a feminist campaigner in the UK[87] created a report button for abusive tweets, after having earlier resisted adding this functionality.[88]

Conclusion

What this chapter has covered is a review of the landscape of international and regional laws, and the situation of transnational Internet intermediary companies. Different definitions of hate speech are evident within this patchwork of international instruments, and these are also applied differently by governmental actors and private companies. While privilege should be given by all actors to the several norms in universal treaties, the practical reality is much more variegated and complicated by the relative autonomy of Internet intermediaries and their major role in online communications.

This report now turns to examine the social responses to perceived hate speech on online platforms.

5. ANALYSING SOCIAL RESPONSES

In the aftermath of dramatic incidents, calls for more restrictive or intrusive measures to contain the Internet's potential to spread hate and violence are common, as if the links between online and offline violence were well known. On the contrary, as the following example indicates, appearances may often be deceiving.

Stormfront is considered the first "hate website" (Meddaugh and Kay, 2009). Launched in March 1995 by a former Ku Klux Klan leader, it quickly became a popular space for discussing ideas related to Neo-Nazism, White nationalism and White separatism, first in the USA and then globally (Bowman-Grieve, 2009). The forum hosts ignominious views, including calls for a racial holy war and incitement to use violence to resist immigration (Bowman-Grieve, 2009) and is considered a space for recruiting activists and possibly coordinating violent acts. The few studies that have explored who the users of *Stormfront* actually are, however, depict a more complex picture. Rather than seeing it as a space for coordinating actions, well-known extreme right activists have accused the forum to be just a gathering for "keyboard warriors". One of them for example, as reported by De Koster and Houtman, stated, "I have read quite a few pieces around the forum, and it strikes me that a great fuss is made, whereas little happens. The section activism/politics itself is plainly ridiculous. [...] Not to mention the assemblies where just four people turn up' (De Koster and Houtman, 2008). Even more revealing are some of the responses to these accusations provided by regular members of the website. As one of them argued, "Surely, I am entitled to have an opinion without actively carrying it out. [...] I do not attend demonstrations and I neither join a political party. If this makes me a keyboard warrior, that is all right. I feel good this way. [...] I am not ashamed of it' (De Koster and Houtman, 2008). De Koster and Houtman surveyed only one national chapter of Stormfront and a non-representative sample of users, but answers like those above should at least invite to caution towards hypotheses connecting expressions and actions, even in spaces whose main function is to host extremist views.

Against this backdrop, the analysis in the next sections seeks to offer a nuanced picture of how concerns about hate speech and violence can be matched with a range of responses. The first section focuses on efforts to respond to the potential of hate speech online, and develop early warning systems and methods to distinguish among different typologies of speech acts. Section two examines coordinated actions by members of the civil society seeking to create national and international coalitions to address emergent threats connecting hatred and violence. The third section offers examples of how pressure groups have interacted with social networking platforms and other Internet intermediaries to offer more robust responses to hate speech online. The fourth and final section focuses on media and information literacy and how it has been embraced by educational organizations, local authorities and other institutions to prepare users to interpret and react to hateful messages.

Monitoring and discussing hate speech

The climate for hate speech is likely to become the most conducive in situations where the political stakes are high, such as during elections. Rumours and accusations before election-day may create the pre-conditions for calls to violence. This section analyses the broader issues arising from practical responses developed to deal with the potential of online hate speech emerging in such situations. One response that provides a backdrop for wider observations is the *UMATI* research project, which began in September 2012, ahead of the Kenyan elections of March 2013, monitoring Kenyan online discourse in order to estimate both the occurrence and virulence of hate speech. The experiences provided different stakeholders an opportunity to analyse the issues, its targets and to collectively reflect on the potential specific speech acts have to lead to violence. The significance of this initiative can be seen in terms of the observation by the UN Human Rights Council Special Rapporteur on Minority Issues: "Few countries collect data on hate crimes, their causes and victims that would enable policy-makers to better protect population groups at risk" (HRC, 2015)

In 2007, Kenya held the most contested, and most violent, elections since it returned to multiparty-ism in 1991, leaving more than 1,000 people dead and 600,000 displaced.[89] Many were taken by surprise that a country that had been praised for its vibrant political scene and economic prosperity could witness such levels of conflict. Others pointed at the deep-rooted tensions (Kanyinga, 2009). This was the first election where new ICTs became an integral part of the electoral contest (Cheeseman, 2008). Social media, emails and SMS text messages were used to unprecedented extents to rally supporters and disseminate information, but also to spread rumours. In the most divided places, such as in urban slums, rumours became an essential component in the narration of the events, with individuals belonging to different political and ethnic groups suggesting how their opponents were planning actions to attack, kill, and evict individuals and communities (Osborn, 2008). Documents were forged and disseminated online to cast doubts on presidential candidates. The role of ICTs continued during the post-election period when both old and new media were used to disseminate calls to violence and coordinate actions (Sommerville, 2011). In the wake of the violence, Kenya set up the National Cohesion and Integration Commission which worked with media and with law enforcement officials to counter the problems of ethnic tensions.

Cognizant of this background, a group of researchers and entrepreneurs came together ahead of Kenya's next electoral competition in 2013 and launched UMATI (which means "crowd" in Kiswahili), a project seeking to monitor online instances of hate speech. UMATI's overall goal was to detect signals of any tensions that may be mounting among Kenyan citizens in order to offer a picture of the major fault lines characterizing different phases of the electoral contest, and to sound the alarm before it was too late.

The elections took place in March 2013, and the project lasted for nine months between September 2012 and May 2013. It tracked blogs, forums, online newspapers and Facebook and Twitter content generated by Kenyans in English as well in the major languages spoken in Kenya, including Kikuyu, Luhya, Kalenjin, Luo, Kiswahili, Sheng (a slang spoken mostly in urban areas), and Somali. Adopting the definition of dangerous speech elaborated by Susan Benesch (2012) as a subset of hate speech with the highest potential to catalyse violence, the UMATI team defined practical criteria to discern among different speech acts and weight their potential to catalyse violence. Monitors evaluated questions based on the influence the speaker had upon the online community, the content of the statement, and the social and historical context that the speech occurred in. As a result of the combination of these criteria, speech acts could be sorted into three different categories: offensive speech, moderately dangerous speech, and dangerous speech. The daily monitoring, the possibility to position different speech acts along a continuum and the mapping of other variables, including the targets of hate speech and whether speech acts referred to specific events, allowed the research to monitor the evolution of hate speech over time and offer a more nuanced understanding of the real and perceived risks.

The findings of the UMATI project, when mapped onto the cases of violence, or lack thereof, during Kenya's 2013 elections, offer a wider indication of the complexities of linking online speech with actions offline. Differently from the previous electoral context, the 2013 elections were in fact largely peaceful. This does not mean that hate speech was less abrasive or widespread. Despite the absence of a baseline that could allow clear comparisons, in 2013 the UMATI project still identified serious, extensive and ongoing cases of hate speech and calls to violence (iHub Research, 2013). These speech acts, however, did not directly translate into violence on the ground. As the team suggested, other factors are likely to have played a more significant part in accounting for the incidence of violent or indeed peaceful outcomes. The numerous calls to peace, coming from different corners of society, including the media, religious groups, politicians on different sides of the political spectrum created a climate where acts of violence were severely condemned (iHub Research, 2013).

The UMATI project also offered the opportunity to test how public perceptions of hate speech compared with those used among scholars and in policy circles. As a result of a survey conducted among Kenyans, the project illustrated that the majority of those who participated in the research considered personal insults, propaganda, and negative commentary about politicians as hate speech. They similarly held a broader conceptualisation of hate speech than what is stated in Kenya's 2010 Constitution, which in Article 33 prohibits "propaganda for war, incitement to violence, hate speech or advocacy of hatred that constitutes ethnic incitement, vilification of others or incitement to cause harm". As Nanjira Sambuli, UMATI's Project Lead explained, the awareness of how hate speech was conceptualized by Kenyans offers an opportunity for discussing not just what hate speech means, but also to place it into a broader context. As she stated:

> The media were asking us to go on air and discuss hate speech. And we had to explain the differences between speech that can cause harm and simple insults against political leaders. But this was also an opportunity for having broader discussions on freedom of expression. So we were invited to talk about hate speech, but then we ended up talking about freedom.[90]

Finally, the project offered some indications on how different social networking platforms may enable distinct ways for hate messages to spread and to be counteracted. Only 3% of the total hate speech comments collected by Umati originated on Twitter, while 90% were found on Facebook. UMATI's final report offers some indications of why this could be the case. As it explains

> Facebook architecture allows for conversations to be formed around a particular topic, and more so, to continue to exist around that topic. This is made possible through Facebook threads, groups and pages, all of which have independent lifespans. In contrast, on Twitter, topics have a lifespan that is dependent on popularity. Through the use of hash tags, the most discussed topics become 'trending topics' and consequently gain more exposure across Twitter. However, when a more popular topic arises, it stands the chance of overshadowing the current trending topic, thereby ending its lifespan. Unlike on Twitter, Facebook groups and pages allow for topics to exist independent of any activity on them" (iHub Research, 2013).

Facebook's architecture also allows users to engage in different behaviours on different spaces. A user may have a "clean" timeline on his or her personal profile, while still posting hateful messages on specific groups and pages. On Twitter, on the contrary, all the user's posts are contained in a singular information domain, and can be viewed by everyone that follows the user.

When it comes to challenging hate speech, the project showed how different platforms also allowed different, and variably effective, responses. In many instances, tweets that were considered unacceptable were shunned and their authors publicly ridiculed. In some cases the 'offender' was even forced to retract statements due to the crowd's feedback, or to close his/her Twitter account altogether. As the report concluded "the singular conversation stream architecture found on Twitter facilitates [this type of response] since all posts are contained on a single timeline and can be viewed by all" (iHub Research, 2013). Similar responses were found to be less likely to occur on Facebook, as the platform's architecture tends to make conversations more stove-piped and less accessible to broad audiences.

This study does not extensively look at the role of the news media in regard to hate speech, given that reportage of such speech generally does not amount to advocacy of incitement to discrimination, hostility or violence, but is a service in the public interest. Nevertheless, news media institutions still frequently encounter the need to identify and respond to speech contributed by users to their online platforms – such as in comment sections on articles, or display feeds of live text messages or tweets. There are different systems in operation and a range of practices that have been analysed in depth in two studies. One is a review of legal and institutional dispensations in South East Europe by the Albanian Media Institute, which also provides advice for optimum self-regulatory practices. The second study is titled "Online comment moderation: emerging best practices", produced by the World Association of Newspapers and which analyses the practices of 104 news organisations from 63 countries (Goodman and Cherubini, 2013). For news media to deal with dynamic flows of user messages, without restricting legitimate expression, is a challenge that begins with the need for policies as to what each institution itself will define as hate speech as a foundation for what calibrated responses may be called for – including responses that encourage counter-speech and discussion of hate speech. Operational routines are needed – as indeed is the case in relation to talk radio that hosts listener phone-ins. All this requires a monitoring system by each media house, even if this is a minimal mechanism for readers to flag and report incidents for further investigation by the platform's editors. Practices of monitoring and discussion of hate speech online in the news media could be profitably shared with Internet intermediary companies, notwithstanding the different standing of these two entities.

Mobilizing civil society

Experience in Myanmar provides an example of positive responses that civil society can elaborate to raise awareness and counteract voices of hatred. The country is transitioning towards greater openness and access to the Internet has grown at unprecedented rates. In this context, however, social media have often been used by some to spread calls to violence.[91] In 2014, the UN Human Rights Council Special Rapporteur on Minority Issues expressed her concern over the spread of misinformation, hate speech and incitement to violence, discrimination and hostility in the media and Internet, particularly targeted against a minority community (HRC, 2015). The growing tension online has gone parallel with cases of actual violence leaving hundreds dead and thousands displaced, although, as pointed out throughout this study, it would be simplistic to seek direct causal relationships between the online speech and the actual acts.[92]

After passing a new constitution in 2008 and holding elections in 2010, Myanmar embarked on a new path towards greater openness and social inclusion. The government led by President Thein Sein, a former military commander, has allowed reforms in key sectors, including the media, where unprecedented spaces for debate have been able to grow. In 2013 only 1.2% of the population had access to the Internet, and little more than 12% to the mobile phone (in 2009, this percentage was lower than 1%). However, the two companies that have won contracts to develop Myanmar ICT infrastructure, Qatari Ooredoo and Norwegian Telenor, have pledged they will reach more 90% mobile coverage in five years.[93]

One challenge in this process has concerned ethnic and religious minorities. In 2013, 43 people were killed due to clashes that erupted after a dispute in the Rakhine state in the Western Part of the country.[94] A year earlier, more than 200 people were killed and thousands displaced because of ethnic violence, which erupted after an alleged rape case.[95] Against this backdrop, the rapid emergence of new online spaces, albeit for a fraction of the population, has reflected some of these deeply rooted tensions in a new form. Dealing with intolerance and hate speech online is an emerging issue.

Facebook has rapidly become the platform of choice for those citizens making their first steps online. In this environment there have been individual and groups, which have championed a more aggressive use of the medium, especially when feeling protected by a sense of righteousness and by claims to be acting in defence of the national interest. Political figures have also used online media for particular causes. In social media, there has been the use of derogatory terms in reference to minorities.[96]

In this complex situation, a variety of actors has begun to mobilize, seeking to offer responses that can avoid further violence. Facebook has sought to take a more active role in monitoring the uses of the social network platform in Myanmar, developing partnerships with local organizations and making guidelines on reporting problems accessible in Burmese.[97] Myanmar's Information Minister Ye Htut has pledged to take further steps to fight hate speech online and has expressed his government's interest in developing stronger ties with the USA to find effective measures to contain online hate speech.[98] It is the creative responses from the local civil society that are analysed below.

The local civil society has constituted a strong voice in openly condemning the spread of online hate speech, but at the same time calling for alternatives to censorship. Among the most innovative responses has been Panzagar, which in Burmese means "flower speech", a campaign launched by blogger and activist Nay Phone Latt to openly oppose hate speech. The goal of the initiative was offering a joyful example of how people can interact, both online and offline. Flowers have a powerful meaning in Myanmar. As Nay Phone Latt explained, "If the public gets the message, they will oppose those who are using dangerous hate speech. Also, we want to gradually convince the extremist groups who are spreading the hate speech to stop".[99] The campaign encouraged Facebook users to update their profile with a picture of them holding a flower in their mouths.

The campaign received significant attention, both at the national and international level, but, as some of the activists interviewed for this study recognized, there is awareness that campaigns need take root among those living in the rural areas and among the least educated. Winning coalitions need to be created, and widely respected religious leaders need to be rallied. In addition, there is sensitivity to not just encouraging "flower speech", but also denouncing the violence. Activists express awareness of the need to clarify the limits of what can and what cannot be said, and the role of the state in tackling the problem.

While initiatives such as Panzagar have been able to rally different groups together, civil society groups are not necessarily unanimous on the solutions to the problem of hate speech. Myat Ko Ko, for example, indicated how there are different, and sometimes, contrasting opinions among civil society groups. Some are against laws that would more strictly punish hate speech; some are in favour. At the same time, he stated,

> "They are afraid that hate speech can be a danger for a peaceful transition. They are aware that the country is fragile." He continued, "If the response comes from the civil society, the civil society will own it. It will be in control. If the response is the law, it will be the state to control it".[100]

Local activists have been focussed upon local solutions, rather than trying to mobilize global civil society on these issues. This is in contrast to some other online campaigns that have been able to attract the world's attention towards relatively neglected problems. Initiatives such as those promoted by the *Save Darfur Coalition* for the civil war in Sudan, or the organization *Invisible Children* with the Kony2012 campaign that denounced the atrocities committed by the Lord Resistance Army, are popular examples. As commentaries on these campaigns have pointed out, such global responses may have negative repercussions on the ability for local solutions to be found (Schomerus, 2012).

The case of Myanmar is an example of how civil society organizations can proactively mobilize and create local coalitions that are able to address emergent threats. Harry Myo Lin, a Panzagar activist, explains,

> Right now we want to concentrate on working with monastic schools, but also with Muslim clerics. It is a process that will take a long time, but we do not want to focus only on hate speech in the social media.[101]

As the activists interviewed for the study recognized, the balance between local focus, raising international attention, producing locally relevant results, and avoiding upsetting a delicate transition is fragile. However, their efforts show that a mobilization against online hatred may be an opportunity to use the Internet among their tactics to address conflicts that are being reflected online.

Lobbying private companies

Various organizations that have been combating hate speech in other forms or that have been defending the rights of specific groups in the past have found themselves playing an increasingly important role online. This is especially evident in developed countries where Internet penetration is high, and where private companies are the key intermediaries. This section examines campaigns and initiatives in the USA, Australia and the United Kingdom, where issues of online hatred have emerged with regard to religion, race and gender. The section highlights the wider significance of how these responses have dealt with cases of perceived hate speech.

Different strategies to act

Organizations like the USA-based *Anti-Defamation League* (ADL), the *Women, Action and the Media* (WAM!), the Australian-based *Online Hate Prevention Institute*, the Canada-based *Sentinel Groups for Genocide Prevention*, and the British-based *Tell Mama-Measuring Anti-Muslim Attacks* have become increasingly invested in combating hate speech online by targeting Internet intermediaries and asking them to take greater responsibility in moderating content, and by trying to raise awareness among users.

> Christopher Wolf, one of ADL's board members, has affirmed that, "It appears that people exposed to online hate speech today seem to just shrug their shoulders and move on because they have gotten used to it, they have grown numb. We don't have enough online education literacy; individuals are just given the devices and use them without any clear guidance, and I think we can do better than that in terms of education."[102]

The need for improved education and accessible information to counter online hate speech has also been advocated by the Sentinel Project for Genocide Prevention's director of operations, Drew Boyd, who concluded that, "Ignorance is a common thread connecting online and offline hate speech. The lack of information either intentionally or unintentionally leads to people adopting narrow worldviews that may accommodate hateful views of others. There is a need for a collaborative effort in spreading information that will reveal facts and other world views to closed collaborative networks of information which circle false or misguided information."[103]

Aside from sensitising users, these groups also focus on putting pressure on Internet intermediaries to act more strongly against hate speech online. Their actions can be divided into two, often complementary, strategies:

In some cases, organizations have focused on directly lobbying private companies by picking up specific, ad-hoc cases and entering in negotiations. This process may involve these organizations promoting their cases through online campaigns, organized barrages of complaints, open letters, online petitions and active calls for supporters' mobilization both online and offline. However, it is the organizations that largely drive a specific cause. This is the case, for example, of the request to Google to modify its search criteria to avoid including *Jew Watch*, an anti-Semitic website promoting holocaust denial, among its top results when searching for the word "Jew" (Foxman & Wolf 2013), and is also the case of the campaign promoted by WAM! described below.

A second type of initiative promoted by some of these organizations is collecting complaints from users about specific types of content. This activity appears particularly interesting when considered in relation to the process adopted by Internet intermediaries to solve cases of hate speech. While companies like Google, for example, have begun to publish public transparency reports listing requests that governments advance for data, information, and content to be disclosed or removed, they have not released information about requests coming from individual users. When individuals flag content as inappropriate, they may be notified about the processing status their complaints (in the case of Facebook for example they can do so through a dedicated dashboard), but this process remain largely hidden to other users and organizations. This has the result of limiting the possibility of developing a broader understanding of what individuals deem to be offensive, inappropriate, insulting, or hateful speech.

Examples of initiatives crowdsourcing requests to take action against specific types of messages include *HateBase*, promoted by The Sentinel Group for Genocide Prevention and Mobiocracy, Tell Mama's *Islamophobic incidents reporting platform*, and the Online Hate Prevention Institute's *Fight Against Hate*. These initiatives take combating online hate speech a step further and serve as innovative tools for keeping track of hate speech across social networks and how it is being regulated by different private companies.

HateBase focuses on mapping hate speech in publically available messages on social networking platforms in order to provide a geographical map of the hateful content disseminated online. This allows for both a global overview and a more localized focus on specific language used and popular hate trends and targets. This database also consists of a complementary individual reporting function utilized to improve the accuracy and scope of analysis by having users verifying examples of hate speech online and confirming their hateful nature in a given community.[104] Similarly, Fight Against Hate allows for reporting online hate speech on different social networks in one platform, which also helps users keep track of how many people report the hate content, where they come from, how long it has taken private companies to respond to the reports and whether the content was effectively moderated.[105] Finally, Tell Mama, a United Kingdom-based organization, offers a similar function of multiple site reporting in one platform, yet focuses solely on anti-Muslim content. This reporting platform also facilitates the documentation of incidents on racial and religious backgrounds for later analysis. The reports received on the platform are processed by the organization, which then contacts victims and helps them deal with the process of reporting certain incidents to the appropriate law enforcements authorities.[106] The information recorded is also used to detect trends in online and offline hate speech against Muslims in the UK.[107]

In discussing the importance of generating empirical data, the Online Hate Prevention Institute's CEO, Andre Oboler stated that platforms like these offer the possibility to make requests visible to other registered users allowing them to keep track of when the content is first reported, how many people report it and how long it takes on average to remove it.

Through these and other means, these organizations may become part of wider coalitions of actors participating in a debate on the need to balance between freedom of expression and respect for human dignity. This is well illustrated in the example below, where a Facebook page expressing hatred against Aboriginal Australians was eventually taken down by Facebook even if it did not openly infringe its terms of service, but because it was found to be insulting by a broad variety of actors, including civil society and pressure groups, regulators, and individual users.

Long-haul campaigning

This case illustrates how a large-scale grassroots controversy surrounding online hate speech can reach concerned organizations and government authorities, which then actively engage in the online debate and pressure private companies to resolve an issue related to hate speech online. In 2012, a Facebook page mocking indigenous Australians called "Aboriginal Memes" caused a local online outcry in the form of an organized flow of content abuse reports, vast media coverage, an online social campaign and an online petition with an open letter demanding that Facebook removes the content. Memes refer in this case to a visual form for conveying short messages through a combination of pictures with inscriptions included in the body of the picture.

The vast online support in the struggle against the "Aboriginal Meme" Facebook page was notable across different social media and news platforms, sparking further interest among foreign news channels as well. In response to the media commotion, Facebook released an official statement on the Australian media saying, "We recognize the public concern that controversial meme pages that Australians have created on Facebook have cause. We believe that sharing information, and the openness that results, invites conversation, debate and greater understanding. At the same time, we recognize that some content that is shared may be controversial, offensive or even illegal in some countries."[108] In response to Facebook's official statement, the Australian Human Rights Commissioner interviewed on public television asserted his disapproval of the controversial page and of the fact that Facebook was operating according the First Amendment to the U.S. Constitution on a matter that involved both an Australian-based perpetrator and Australian-based victims.[109]

The online petition was established as a further response to Facebook's refusal to remove the content by automatically answering several content abuse reports with the statement, "After reviewing your report, we were not able to confirm that the specific page you reported violates Facebook's Statement of Rights and Responsibilities".[110] The open letter in the petition explained that it viewed the content as offensive due to repeated attacks against a specific group on racist grounds and demanded that Facebook take action by removing the specific pages in question and other similar pages that are aimed against indigenous Australians. In August 11th, 2012, the founder of the petition, Jacinta O'Keefe, published a note in which she thanked the participants and announced the petition's victory when she discovered that Facebook had removed the said content and another hateful page targeting indigenous Australians.[111] However, the pages had only been removed temporarily for content review and after talks with the Race Discrimination Commissioner and the Institute, Facebook concluded that the content did not violate its terms of services and allowed the pages to continue under the requirement of including the word "controversial" in its title to clearly indicate that the page consisted of controversial content.[112]

A second content regulation phase came after a Facebook user began targeting online anti-hate activists with personal hate speech attacks due to the "Aboriginal Memes" case. Facebook responded by tracing and banning the numerous fake users established by the perpetrator, yet allowed him to keep one account operational. Finally, in a third phase, Facebook prevented access to the debated page within Australia following publically expressed concerns by both the Race Discrimination Commissioner and the Australian Communications and Media Authority. However, the banned Facebook page remains operational and accessible outside of Australia, and continues to spread hateful content posted in other pages that are available in Australia. Some attempts to restrict specific users further disseminating the controversial 'Aboriginal Memes' resulted with a 24-hour ban from using Facebook. These measures were criticised as ineffective deterrents (Oboler, 2012).

Campaigning targeting advertisers

In this case, the organizations involved took up a long-standing online controversy and went beyond serving as intermediaries for complaints by themselves actively and aggressively lobbying companies, demanding closer content moderation and further, permanent self-regulatory action. In 2013, Women, Action and the Media group (WAM!)[113] and the Everyday Sexism Project in the UK[114] took an aggressive public relations approach and launched a shared campaign showing page advertisements of prominent companies in Facebook pages that disseminated graphic content that was abusive of women. In response to the campaign, both Nissan and the insurance company Nationwide pulled out their advertisements from Facebook. Upon seeing their success, the organizers, backed up by online supporters and activists began sending written complaints and photos of different advertisements in hateful pages to other major companies like Dove and American Express on their social media platforms, urging them to follow suit. As a result of this campaign, 15 major companies decided to remove their adverts from Facebook.[115]

The campaign also included an official open letter written by the two aforementioned groups listing pages that promoted rape and violence against women and demanding that the pages be removed and that Facebook revise its content regulation policy. Alongside the open letter, an online petition on change.org collected over 225,000 signatures and helped raise awareness among online users.[116] Activists supporting the campaign decided to take further action and initiated a large scale protest in front of Facebook's shareholder meeting, publishing the name of all prominent companies using the platform for online advertising and calling on people to send them letters of complaints and urging them to withdraw their advertisements from Facebook. Furthermore, activists also engaged financial writers in their social media pages, asking them to analyse the potential fiscal damage Facebook could endure due to the growing number of companies pulling out. The online campaign using the Hashtag #FBrape against Facebook and companies advertising in the platform resulted in Facebook contacting the organizations concerned in a request for cooperation. The #FBrape campaign only gained notable media attention after it was successful in pressuring the company into an active fight against hateful content targeting women, mostly because it was a swift blow that targeted specific companies and their advertising campaigns rather than just Facebook directly.[117]

Facebook's response, however, was not as cooperative initially, as it maintained that the pages listed in the open letter did not violate the company's terms of service. Yet shortly after the campaign began and companies started pulling out, the offensive content was quickly removed. Facebook then released an official statement on its website, stating that they wished to clarify their terms of services and content regulation policies, and also promote cooperation with organizations working to promote freedom of speech while preventing online hate speech from targeting specific groups and individuals. At the end of the letter Facebook added, "In recent days, it has become clear that our systems to identify and remove hate speech have failed to work as effectively as we would like, particularly around issues of gender-based hate. In some cases, content is not being removed as quickly as we want. In other cases, content that should be removed has not been or has been evaluated using outdated criteria".[118] The company then declared that it intended to review and update its guidelines concerning hate speech moderation, provide its content moderators with better quality training, strengthen its collaboration with concerned organizations to facilitate a shared, responsive effort to better counter hateful content online and also act to hold distributers of such offensive content accountable for such actions.[119]

In a separate, yet related instance, Twitter also took a stand against online harassment of women in collaboration with WAM!, by launching a joint pilot project in the form of a reporting platform that would attempt to moderate the content reported within 24 hours. The reports filed by victims of online abuse of women are aimed to serve a dual purpose: allowing WAM!

to collect data on offensive content focused on gender-based online harassment in order to explore the phenomenon in depth; and helping Twitter improve its content regulation mechanisms in relation to gender-based online discrimination and abuse.[120] The reporting tool asks women to name the specific users harassing them or the specific tweets they find offensive, classify the type of harassment and answer general questions about how many times they have been harassed, on which platforms and whether the harassment came from one or multiple users. After the report is filed, the claims are investigated by WAM! and then passed to Twitter for further investigation and moderation.[121]

Twitter issued a statement about its efforts to combat online hate speech, advocating that, "We are always trying to improve the way we handle abuse issues, and WAM! is one of many organizations we work with around the world on best practices for user safety".[122] WAM!'s executive director, Jaclyn Friedman stressed the importance of the initiative, saying, "We are thrilled to be working with Twitter to make their platform safer for women. The disproportionate targeting of women online results in them removing their voices from public conversation. We are so glad that Twitter recognizes that the best way to ensure equally free speech for all users on their platform is to ensure that all users are equally free to speak without being targeted by harassment, abuse and threats".[123] The pilot program for the reporting tool has operated for three weeks, in which it claimed to have gathered 700 reports and helped over 100 people get faster responses from Twitter. The organization plans to produce a report on the data gathered in the process, aimed at attaining a better understanding of online hate speech against women.[124]

Limitations in combating hate speech online and responses by Internet intermediaries

It appears that the fight against perceived online hate speech is beginning to reach a number of concerned parties, from governments to private companies and Internet Service Providers, as well as to a growing number of active organizations and affected individuals. There are also many online communities and individuals fighting against hateful content online on a daily basis alongside more formal organizations. However, this fight necessitates large-scaled action in order to ensure that online hate speech can be effectively and contextually identified and remedied in the long run, and it requires empowerment of users to identify and combat hate speech without blocking legitimate speech, and in this way creating more inclusive spaces for expression.

Internet intermediaries and social networking platforms in particular have advanced their responses to alleged hate speech online through careful interactions with user complaints and by increasingly making their regulation process more transparent. In an interview with Monika Bickert and Ciara Lyden[125] from Facebook, they indicated they rely on multiple teams dealing with different types of content in different languages in order to address reported content as quickly and as effectively as possible. Furthermore, Facebook has introduced a reporting dashboard that allows users to keep track of the reviewing process of their reports in order to improve their individual communications with each user. Adopting similar mechanisms to contend with hateful speech, Twitter introduced a report button in 2013[126] following an online petition set up by an individual user.[127]

In summary, internet intermediaries are increasingly working in close cooperation with different organizations to provide rapid and effective responses to hate speech on their platforms, yet they also emphasize that they equally weigh complaints by individuals and treat these as seriously as they do petitions and other forms of collective action. Finally, these private companies are also beginning to issue transparency reports in order to inform users of any changes in their policies and privacy settings, although few provide information about user reports in comparison to official governments requests.[128]

Countering online hate speech through media and information literacy

While the previous sections have addressed mostly reactive responses to the proliferation of hate speech online, this section offers insights on attempts to provide more structural answers to hate speech online through education. It analyses a series of initiatives targeting the youth or partnering with educational institutions to make them aware of the issues around and possible responses to perceived hate speech online.

Citizenship education and digital citizenship

Citizenship education focuses on preparing individuals to be informed and responsible citizens through the study of rights, freedoms, and responsibilities and has been variously employed in societies emerging from violent conflict (Osler and Starksey, 2005). One of its main objectives is raising awareness on the political, social and cultural rights of individuals and groups, including freedom of speech and the responsibilities and social implications that emerge from it. In some cases, effective argumentation and the skills necessary to articulate personal beliefs and opinions in a respectful way have been included among the learning outcomes established in citizenship education programmes.

The concern of citizenship education with hate speech is twofold: it encompasses the knowledge and skills to identify hate speech, and should enable individuals to counteract messages of hatred. One of its current challenges is adapting its goals and strategies to the digital world, providing not only argumentative but also technological knowledge and skills that a citizen may need to counteract online hate speech. A new concept of digital citizenship is being proposed by some of the organizations included in this study, which incorporates the core objectives of media and information literacy aimed at developing technical and critical skills for media consumers and producers and which connects them with broader ethic and civic matters.

Relevant here is global citizenship education (GCED) is one of the strategic areas of work for UNESCO's Education Programme (2014-2017)[129] and one of the three priorities of the UN Secretary-General's Global Education First Initiative (GEFI) launched in September 2012. Global Citizenship Education aims to equips learners of all ages with those values, knowledge and skills that are based on, and instill respect for, human rights, social justice, diversity, gender equality and environmental sustainability. GCED gives learners the competencies and opportunity to realize their rights and obligations to promote a better world and future for all.

Within this wider perspective, UNESCO also promotes media and information literacy. This is an umbrella concept which covers a package of literacies (on- and off-line). It includes the development of the technical skills and abilities required to use digital technologies as well as the knowledge and abilities needed to find, analyse, evaluate and interpret specific media texts, to create media messages, and to recognise their social and political influence (Hoechsmann and Poyntz, 2012). In recent years, those stressing media literacy have begun to address the social significance of the use of technologies, their ethical implications and the civic rights and responsibilities that arise from their use. Today, information literacy cannot avoid issues such as rights to free expression and privacy, critical citizenship and fostering empowerment for political participation (Mossberger et al. 2008). Multiple and complementary literacies become critical.

The emergence of new technologies and social media has played an important role in this shift. Individuals have evolved from being only consumers of media messages to producers, creators and curator of information, resulting in new models of participation that interact with traditional ones, like voting or joining a political party. Teaching strategies are changing accordingly, from fostering critical reception of media messages to include empowering the creation of media content (Hoechsmann and Poyntz, 2012). The concept of media and information literacy itself continues to evolve, being augmented by the dynamics of the Internet. It is beginning to embrace issues of identity, ethics and rights in cyberspace (See Paris Declaration)[130]

Some of these skills can be particularly important when identifying and responding to hate speech online and the present section analyses a series of initiatives aimed both at providing information and practical tools for Internet users to be active digital citizens. The projects and organisations covered in this type of response are:

- 'No place for hate' by Anti-Defamation League (ADL), USA;

- 'In other words' project by Provincia di Mantova and the European Commission;

- 'Facing online hate' by MediaSmarts, Canada;

- 'No hate speech movement' by Youth Department of the Council of Europe, Europe;[131]

- 'Online hate' by the Online Hate Prevention Institute, Australia.

A comparative outlook on all the listed projects and their materials related to hate speech online was conducted. In addition interviews with representatives of the organisations or people responsible for the educational programmes were conducted.

Education as a tool against hate speech

Even though the initiatives and organisations presented have distinctive characteristics and particular aims, all of them emphasise the importance of media and information literacy and educational strategies as effective means to counteract hate speech. They stress the ability of an educational approach to represent a more structural and viable response to hate speech, considered in comparison to the complexities involved in decisions to ban or censor online content or the time and cost it may take for legal actions to produce tangible outcomes. Many are arguing that the package of competencies within media and information literacy can empower individuals and provide them with the knowledge and skills they need to respond to perceived hate speech in a more immediate way. Such skills can also be particularly important, given the emphasis that social networking platforms are placing on individual reporting of cases of abuse, incitement to hatred, or harassment.

Individuals involved in these initiatives, however, recognise the importance of the legal framework as a reference for their efforts. As Laura Geraghty from the 'No Hate Speech Movement' affirmed:

> Education is key to prevent hate speech online. It is necessary to raise awareness and empower people to get online in a responsible way; however, you still need the legal background and instruments to prosecute hate crimes, including hate speech online, otherwise the preventive aspect won't help.[132]

Most of the initiatives include education about legal instruments and procedures used to prosecute perpetrators of hate speech online, and many encourage a complementary view between legal and the educational aspects. Media literacy and education may represent an increasingly important strategy in countering hate speech online, but, given the extent of the problem, should be considered in relation to other types of responses.

Development of critical skills to counteract hate speech online

A common denominator of the analysed initiatives is the emphasis on the development of critical thinking skills and the ethically-reflective use of social media as starting points of media and information literacy skills to combat hate speech online. The expectation is that these media and information literacy competencies can enhance individuals' ability to identify and question hateful content online, understand some of its assumptions, biases and prejudices, and encourage the elaboration of arguments to confront it.

Not surprisingly, identifying hate speech online is not necessarily as straightforward as it may seem to some. As one teacher participating in a focus group coordinated by MediaSmarts explained:

> It even took me a few minutes before I realized I was on a website that was sympathetic to the Nazis. It was phenomenally written, in evil ways. It cloaked the true racist and hatred messages under prose. You know, using language. And so, I actually had the kids look at it – when my light bulb went off, theirs hadn't yet. They didn't know what they were looking at. I asked them to look a little closer, and some of them started to see it and others still couldn't. And that interested them, because I could see something they couldn't. That was a way for them to see, for them to get interested in the idea that somebody was actually preaching hatred and it didn't even feel like it.[133]

The initiatives analysed are directed towards a diversity of audiences that are involved and affected by online hate speech. For the participant organisations studied here, it is particularly important to focus their efforts on vulnerable groups and on those prone to either being targets of hate or being recruited by hate groups. Children and youth are one of the main audiences targeted by these initiatives. As Matthew Johnson, the Director of Education at MediaSmarts, explained:

> Teaching youth that media are constructions that re-present reality helps make them aware of the need to understand who is behind what they're seeing; teaching them that that media contain ideological messages – about values, power, and authority – which have social and political implications helps them to understand why hate content in music, games or other "trivial" media still needs to be confronted.[134]

Parents, teachers and the school community also tend to be considered an important audience due to their role in exposing and protecting children from hateful content. Other groups are also targeted include those with the ability to shape the legal and political landscape of hate speech online, including policy makers and NGO's, and those who can have a large impact in the online community exposing hate speech, especially journalists, bloggers and activists. A summary of the different audiences targeted in the analysed initiatives can be found on Table 1.

	Children	Youth	Teachers	Parents	Policy makers	Bloggers	NGOs	General audience
Anti-defamation league	X	X	X	X	X			
In Other Words					X	X	X	X
No Hate Speech Movement		X				X		X
MediaSmarts	X	X	X	X				
Online Hate Prevention		X				X	X	X

Table 1. Audiences covered by each educational initiative

As could be expected, not only the content but also the goals and objectives of each project are closely related to the interests and needs of the audience that each initiative aims to reach. For instance, MediaSmarts has developed an online video game for children between 12 to 14 years of age, designed to increase students' ability to recognize bias, prejudice and hate propaganda. In this video game, when they come across varying degrees of prejudice and discrimination, in the form of jokes, news or videos, children are asked to identify how such messages can promote hate and then to develop strategies to deal with them, either by ignoring or confronting them.

The ADL has focused a lot of its outreach and educational efforts on teachers and parents, providing them with essential information on how to discuss hate and violence with children, and how to encourage young people to take the most pertinent action. Leaflets, training sessions in schools and community workshops are examples of the strategies that ADL implements to develop an inclusive culture and respectful school climate.

The No Hate Speech movement has organized training sessions for bloggers and young activists where they can discuss in a friendly environment some of their experiences with hate speech online and share best practices to combat it. For example, how the participants can implement affirmative campaigns that portray minority groups in a positive way to prevent discrimination, or how to conduct obstructive campaigns to report and restrict discriminatory content and activity online.[135] The training sessions aim to promote a grass-root understanding of hate speech and raise awareness on the impact that bloggers and activists can have in tackling hateful content.

In contrast, the project 'In other words' has sought to influence policy makers and civil society to monitor various types of media. This project advocates for the use of accurate information about minorities and vulnerable groups in media representations, encouraging monitoring from society to avoid the dissemination of stereotypes, prejudice and other kinds of discriminatory discourse.

Educational goals of media and information literacy to respond to hate speech

Despite the particularities of the content of each initiative and the audiences that each one addresses, they share three broad educational goals: to inform, to analyse, and to confront hate speech. These three aims can be seen in a continuum encompassing progressive goals with specific objectives, each one focusing on different aspects of the problem and providing specific alternatives to respond to hate online. A summary is shown in Table 2.

Information	Analysis	Action
– Raising awareness about hate speech and its consequences – Conveying and disseminating information – Communicating the relevant legal framework	– Identifying and assessing hate speech – Analyzing common causes and underlying assumptions and prejudices – Recognising biased behaviours – Reporting and exposing hate speech	– Responding to hate speech – Writing against hate speech – Changing the discourse of hate speech – Media monitoring

Table 2. Educational goals and objectives

The first educational goal focuses on conveying information on hate speech, the second on the critical analysis of the phenomenon and a third encourages individuals to take specific actions. Initiatives falling under the scope of information as an educational goal include raising awareness about hate speech online, its different forms and possible consequences. They also provide information on relevant national, regional and international legal frameworks. Examples of these initiatives can be found in multiple formats, for instance the video 'No Hate Ninja Project - A Story About Cats, Unicorns and Hate Speech' by No Hate Speech Movement,[136] the interactive e-tutorial 'Facing online hate' by MediaSmarts[137] or the toolbox developed by the project 'In other words'.[138]

The second educational goal is more complex and focuses on the analysis of hate speech online. This analysis includes assessments and evaluations of the different types of hate speech online, including racism, sexism, and homophobia, and of the multiple forms in which it is presented. An important aspect of the analysis is the critical examination of hate speech in order to identify its common causes and understand its underlying assumptions and prejudices. This analytical process enables individuals to report and expose hateful content online. Examples of projects with this educational goal are the 'No Hate' discussion forum and the 'Reporting hate speech' platform. The discussion forum managed by No Hate Speech Movement allows young people to debate what counts as hateful content and expose some examples of hate speech online that they previously encountered. The following is an extract from a discussion forum:

> A right to express one's mind is an essential human right on the basis of Free Speech, which we all cherish and value[…]. However, there has been a seemingly blurred line between the words used to initiate discussion and the ones used to incite hatred. The phenomenon of mobilising the crowd for violent action by expressing open hostility towards targeted groups has been widely exploited by people in positions to be heard. [139]

Further to the analysis issue, the reporting platform designed by the Online Hate Prevention Institute enables individuals to report and monitor hate speech online, by exposing what they perceive as hate content, tracking websites, forums and groups, and reviewing hateful materials exposed by other people.

Finally, the third educational goal identified in these initiatives focuses on fostering actions that can be taken to combat and counter hate speech acts. Resources within this educational goal aim to promote concrete actions and responses to online hate speech. The actions proposed vary, depending on the focus of the project and the organisation, being more or less combative and confrontational in nature; however, the main focus remains on empowering individuals to respond to and assertively combat hateful content. Examples of these kind of initiatives are training sessions for bloggers, journalists and activists run by the No Hate Speech Movement, the teaching materials and lesson plans developed by MediaSmarts, and the media monitoring policies proposed by the project 'In Other Words'.

Assessing media and information literacy and education initiatives

Whereas some organisations and initiatives focus on the content of hate speech online, others emphasize the personal aspect of it by drawing attention to the victims or to the general impact on the community. Regardless of their focus, most of the projects consider the development of digital skills as an essential aspect to prevent, expose and combat hate speech online. The tools and strategies analysed exhibit a variety of approaches to develop such skills, from basic 'how-to-guides' to more complex and specialised training. The great array of formats discussed and analysed in the different initiatives, including videos, blogs, websites, videogames, and social media, make it possible to reach and attract very different audiences.

Exhaustive evaluations, however, are still lacking, and it is difficult to assess whether and to which extent these initiatives are successful in combating hate speech or affecting groups that are most likely to engage in hate speech online. For instance, even though MediaSmarts' initiatives and resources have received multiple awards and recognitions, there are no clear indications of who makes the most use of their resources and it is difficult to evaluate the results of their programmes. In the case of the project 'In Other Words', the expected results included the development of material for dissemination, but there is no information on how such material has been used since its publication or what audiences it has reached. Also in the case of the 'No Hate Speech Movement', which has developed different materials and resources (including videos, training manuals, educational tools, and the online platform to report hatred content), there are not clear and public guidelines on how to evaluate or report impact.[140] While most of these initiatives are commendable and potentially offer powerful instruments to combat hate speech at a structural level, more information is needed in order to understand how individuals integrate newly acquired skills in their daily lives and routines and what impact this has for their online activity.

6. CONCLUSION AND RECOMMENDATIONS

The emergence and diffusion of hate speech online is an evolving phenomenon and collective efforts are needed to understand its significance and consequences, as well as to develop effective responses. Public displays of indignation have been a common reaction, with some public figures calling for heightened punishments for those spreading hateful messages and stricter controls on Internet communication. As this study has suggested, however, focusing exclusively on repressive measures can miss the complexity of a phenomenon that is still poorly understood and which calls out for tailored and coordinated responses from a range of different actors in society. Online spaces, given their potential to favour interaction, and the fact that they provide unprecedented amounts of data that can be analysed through a variety of new techniques, offer a unique lens into human behaviour. Effective solutions must be grounded in a better understanding of how different forms of expression emerge, interact, and potentially dissipate in this environment.

This study has offered several concrete examples of how different situations have stimulated tailored responses. The emergence of each response is linked to unique circumstances, but their analysis and dissemination offers a general palette of methods that various stakeholders can adapt to different contexts. This concluding chapter summarizes the core findings in ways that can help to address some of the main tensions characterizing hate speech online.

Definition

- The problem of defining hate speech sits at the intersection of multiple contradictions. As highlighted by some of the participants in this study and by processes of the kind of the Rabat Plan of Action, there is an aspiration to elaborate definitions that are widely shared among a broad variety of stakeholders and to develop tests that could indicate what should and what should not be recognized as hate speech. This kind of process enables coordinated responses, although it should recognise that even international institutions have generally **avoided** providing **too stringent definitions**. This caution seems to be shared by some of the most important private players that are shaping online communication. Despite being asked to provide greater clarity on the process through which content moderation takes place, social networking platforms have so far avoided proposing too strict rules and procedures to identify what type of content should be removed. On the contrary, some of them have tried to "socialize" content moderation, allowing users to resolve some controversy through interactions among themselves facilitated by the platform. This allows for nuance and avoids a mechanistic approach.

- Narrower definitions have been advanced, including "**dangerous speech**", which refers to speech acts that have a significant probability of catalysing or amplifying violence by one group against another, or "**fear speech**", which emphasises statements that can incite the fear in one group that "another group" plans to use violence. Concepts like these resonate with legal principles, but rather than being aimed at prosecuting perpetrators, are meant to offer tools to identify and describe particular speech, possibly signalling critical cases or danger zones where collective responses may be needed to avoid the spreading of violence. When it comes to hate speech online, however, all definitions still incur the intractable challenge of making **connections between** the **online expressions** of hatred and **actual harm** such as hostility, discrimination or violence. This is a problem shared by other media, but some of the elements characterizing online communication, including users' real or perceived anonymity, or the immediacy with which a given message may reach wide audiences, make it particularly complex. As the example of Kenya discussed earlier illustrates, online incitements to hatred and calls to violence during the 2013 elections did not translate into actual violence as appears to have been at least partly the case in the previous electoral contest. Other factors, including possibly the numerous calls to peace from different corners of society, seem to have prevailed in this case. As discussed later when dealing with the challenge of *comprehending* hate speech online, this does not mean that connections between online and offline violence cannot be studied and progressively understood, but systematic research is still lacking.

- The emphasis on the **potential** of a speech act to lead to **violence** and cause harm should also be considered for its intrinsic assumptions, which can lead to a narrow approach that is limited to **law and order**. The emphasis on violence points to answers that may privilege the state (as the actor that has the legitimate control of the use of violence), to the possible neglect of other actors that could advance different or complementary solutions. Further, as pointed out at the beginning of this report, hate speech legislation tends to be the expression of the dominant group that controls the content of law. Alternative interpretations of hate speech have focused instead on the respect of human dignity, and empowering the targets of speech acts to demand respect and to be defended, thereby placing them, rather than the state or another actor, at the centre of effective responses. This approach is not devoid of problems and contradictions, as an excessive emphasis on dignity may lead to a cacophony of relativism - or of support for particularistic ideas that are not human rights compliant. But it suggests nevertheless that when addressing hate speech online, different perspectives should be taken into consideration and weighted against one another, both for their ability to explain this phenomenon and its complex link to actual violence, and to offer answers that are not at the expense of a holistic approach.

● Paradoxically, the complexity of defining hate speech offers also opportunities to develop **shared local interpretations** of the different international standards on hate speech. Hate speech operates as a kind of "**empty signifier**" (Laclau and Mouffe, 1985). It is a term that may seem self-explanatory to most, but for which people actually tend to offer very disparate descriptions when asked. This may constitute a problem, for example when accusations of expressing hateful messages are used instrumentally to discredit legitimate speech or to justify cases of censorship. These are instances when criticism or ridicule of individuals, or opinions or beliefs, become labelled as hate speech – despite they go far beyond the parameters spelled out by the ICCPR. The characteristic of the term as an empty signifier, however, may also offer opportunities for different actors to come together and discuss issues that may be difficult to approach otherwise.

Jurisdiction

● Much of the attention towards identifying and responding to hate speech online has concentrated on governments. **Internet intermediaries**, services that mediate online communication, however, have also been playing an increasingly important role both in allowing and constraining expression. Many of them, especially search engines and social networking platforms, stretch across countries and regulate users' interactions based on their own terms of service and definitions of hate speech. They largely rely on users' notifications of content considered inappropriate and when a case is brought to their attention, the default response is to adjudicate it based on their own terms of service. The conditions under which Internet intermediaries operate, however, in terms of how they relate to national and international rules and regulation, pressure groups and individual users, are in constant flux. As this study has indicated, there have been numerous recent instances in which Internet intermediaries have responded to pressures coming from different actors.

● The effect of the 2014 European Court of Justice ruling against Google, where the company now removes, on request, search results on individuals if it judges the information to be irrelevant or outdated, shows the possibility of enforcement of jurisdiction in spaces that for a long time have seemed to escape state power. This **formal** re-territorialization of online spaces, however, is considered particularly controversial. The main reason is that it may lead to a progressive fragmentation of the Internet, with states or groups of states imposing their own rules and breaking down the potential of the Internet to share expression across frontiers and bring people closer to one another. It creates a scenario where the Internet is experienced differently in different localities, and where the norm of free flow becomes overshadowed by national or regional exceptionalism. Private companies themselves and many civil society actors seem to feel particular unease when private institutions are mandated to act as tribunals and decide what should or should not be offered online. There is ongoing debate about the extent to which may differ from voluntary self-regulation, in which companies offer their own channels for individual complainants even though the latter retain the right to resolve a particular concern through the courts if unsuccessful.

● Most Internet intermediaries prefer to take a more **informal** approach to responding to requests coming from governments, groups and individuals. Facebook, for example, has activated a "social reporting" function, which offers users a facility to send a message to a person posting information which the user does not like but which does not violate Facebook's terms of service.[141] Another option is a notice-and-notice facility, whereby individuals, via the intermediary, may demand or contest the removal of particular expression.[142] As this study has shown, there have also been many occurrences of social networking platforms changing or improving the mechanisms through which content is monitored and moderated. These include Twitter ending its resistance to add a report button that can be directly accessed from a tweet. This approach has included degrees of collaboration with governments, but in these cases informality could serve to reduce accountability and transparency both for states and private companies. While informality in some instances responds well to the fluid nature of online hate speech, it has the disadvantage of being ad hoc and piecemeal. In some cases, it may be the particular ability of a pressure group to "hit the right chord" to make the difference, not the importance or validity of a specific cause per se or whether it exceeds international restrictions for the legitimate limitation of expression.

Comprehension

● The objectionable nature of hate messages offers apparently strong justifications for limiting them and silencing their authors such as banning them from a platform or even from use of the Internet. These justifications, notwithstanding that they may be disproportionate and thus fail the "necessity" test for a limitation to be legitimate, tend to grow stronger in the aftermath of dramatic incidents. At such times, authorities may call for strong measures to contain the Internet's potential to spread hate and violence, although the links between online speech and offline violence may be tenuous. In this context, efforts to understand hate speech not solely with the instrumental goal to counter or eliminate it, but also to grasp what it is the expression of, are particularly difficult – yet continue to be very important. This study has described research that investigated **who** the people inhabiting **extremist** online spaces are, **why** they say what they say, and **how** they interpret it, presenting findings that are often counterintuitive.[143] Such studies are still rare, but a **better understanding** of the dynamics that may lead to certain types of speech may offer a much richer picture that can also inform innovative answers not based solely on repressing and silencing. For example, are there links between **economic inequalities** and **hate speech**? How can some people successfully exploit hate speech for partisan ends, and why do many of their victims tend to come from vulnerable or disadvantaged backgrounds?[144] Are there connections between access to **education** and **hate speech**? Answers to questions like these may offer solutions that point towards the need for practical policies for greater social inclusion, rather than actions to solely address hate speech as a symptom of deeper and unexplored grievances.

- Hate speech **online** covers a very broad set of phenomena occurring on different technological platforms. The **architectures** on which these platforms are based, however, may vary significantly and have important repercussions on how hate speech spreads and can be countered. As the UMATI project reported in Chapter 4 indicated, Twitter's architecture made it easier for users to shun those posting hateful messages and calls to violence. The use of hashtags that gather different users around a common issue offer the possibility to share a tweet or a whole account, and allow processes of collective moderation. In the case of Facebook, similar mechanisms are less likely to occur as the platform allows multiple streams of conversations to develop partially hidden from one another. Other platforms, such as Snapchat, reduce the possibility that a message is shared beyond a very close group to a minimum. A more fine-grained understanding how each platform can enable or constrain the production and dissemination of different type of messages may thus be a very important factor in developing appropriate responses.

- Large social networking platforms like Facebook and Twitter have primarily adopted a reactive approach to deal with hateful messages reported by their users, and analysing whether or not they infringed upon their terms of service. Social networking platforms could, however, take a **more proactive approach**. They have access to a tremendous amount of data that can be correlated, analysed, and combined with real life events that would allow more nuanced understanding of the dynamics characterizing hate speech online. Vast amount of data are already collected and correlated for marketing purposes. Similar efforts could be made as part of the social responsibility mandate of the companies owning these platforms, contributing to produce knowledge that can be shared with a broad variety of stakeholders.

- Initiatives promoting greater **media and information literacy** have begun to emerge as a more structural response to hate speech online. Given young people's increasing exposure to social media, information about how to identify and react to hate speech may become increasingly important. While some schools have expressed interest in progressively incorporating media and information literacy in their curriculum, these initiatives, however, are still patchy and have often not reached the most vulnerable who need the most to be alerted about the risk of hate speech online and offline. It is particularly important that anti-hate speech modules are incorporated in those countries where the actual risk of widespread violence is highest. There is also a need to include in such programmes, modules that reflect on identity, so that young people can recognise attempts to manipulate their emotions in favour of hatred, and be empowered to advance their individual right to be their own masters of who they are and wish to become. Pre-emptive and preventative initiatives like these should also be accompanied by measures to evaluate the impact upon students' actual behaviour online and offline, and on their ability to identify and respond to hate speech messages.

Intervention

- The problem of hate speech online demands **collective solutions**. This may seem an obvious conclusion and one that is shared by many other areas of social life. As this study has indicated, however, there are peculiar elements to the issue of hate speech online that are likely to make responses entrusting only one or a limited number of actors highly ineffective.

- The **Internet** stretches **across borders** and despite repeated attempts by states to reaffirm their sovereignty also in the digital domain, complex problems like responding to hate speech online cannot be easily addressed simply by relying upon state power. For example, identifying and prosecuting all individuals posting hateful messages would be impractical for most states.

- As proposed by the UN Human Rights Council Special Rapporteur on Minority Issues, **States** could work collaboratively with organisations and projects that conduct campaigns to combat hate speech, including on the Internet, including by providing financial support (HRC, 2015).

● **Internet intermediaries**, on their part, have an interest in maintaining a relative independence and a "**clean**" **image**. They have sought to reach this goal by demonstrating their responsiveness to pressures from civil society groups, individuals and governments. The way in which these negotiations have occurred, however, have been so far been ad hoc, and they have not led to the development of collective over-arching principles.

● As some of the individuals interviewed for this study have suggested, many users seem to have been **numbed** by the incidence and presence of **hate speech online**. More structural initiatives are needed in order to explain not only how certain instances can be reported, but also why this is important in creating shared spaces where dialogue can occur around hate speech. There also seems to be potential to consolidate the silent or passive middle ground to lean away from hateful extremes, by activists engaging with online hate speech through the medium of counter speech.[145]

● Defining hate speech online will probably continue to escape a universally observed consensus for a long time, but a range of engagements with it can nevertheless be developed on a multistakeholder **basis**. It is clear that no single actor can solve the problem of online hate speech, irrespective of how the phenomenon is defined. Ongoing participative processes of comprehension of the nature of online hate speech are as important as the evolving responses.

Authors and Acknowledgements

Iginio Gagliardone is Research Fellow in New Media and Human Rights in the Centre for Socio-Legal Studies and a member of the Programme in Comparative Media Law and Policy (PCMLP) at the University of Oxford. His research and publications focus on media and political change, particularly in Sub-Saharan Africa, and on the emergence of distinctive models of the information society worldwide. He is also a research associate of the Oxford Internet Institute, the Centre of Governance and Human Rights at the University of Cambridge, and the Centre for Global Communication Studies at the Annenberg School of Communication, University of Pennsylvania.

Danit Gal, currently based at the Oxford Internet Institute at the University of Oxford, specializes in Cyber Security and Information Warfare. Danit has carried out extensive research on extremist propaganda and communications online as an Argov Fellow and Ragonis Foundation Scholar at the Interdisciplinary Center Herzliya, Israel.

Thiago Alves Pinto is currently conducting research for his DPhil in Law at the University of Oxford. He has worked for the United Nations Special Rapporteur on Freedom of Religion or Belief and the International Organization for Migration in Finland on counter trafficking and development projects.

Gabriela Martínez Sainz is a DPhil Candidate at University of Cambridge. She is researching human rights education in Mexico, with a view to integrate theory and professional practices applying gained knowledge to the development of educational and training programmes for human rights educators. She is author of textbooks on citizenship and ethics education for secondary school children in Mexico.

The authors are deeply grateful to the many people who have contributed to the development of this study. We are indebted to the many interviewees who found time to speak with us, sometimes on multiple occasions and despite their many commitments. We have been very fortunate to rely on an impressive advisory board, whose members have provided guidance and feedback as the report developed, including Monroe Price, Richard Danbury, Cherian George, Nazila Ghanea, Robin Mansell, Bitange Ndemo, and Nicole Stremlau. We are also grateful to the many people at UNESCO who have been providing comments to earlier versions of this report, helping to strengthen it and ensure it can contribute to wider debates on freedom online.

List of works cited

Albanian Media Institute. 2014. *Hate speech in online media in South East Europe.* http://www.institutemedia. org/Documents/PDF/Hate%20speech%20in%20online%20media%20in%20SEE.pdf

Aung, S. Y. 2014. 'Hate Speech Pours Poison Into the Heart' http://www.irrawaddy.org/interview/hate-speech-pours-poison-heart.html

Australian Copyright Council. 2013. *Websites: Social Networks, Blogs and user generated content.* Information sheet G108v03, June 2013.

Benesch, S. 2012. Dangerous Speech: A Proposal to Prevent Group Violence, World Policy Institute, New York, no. 2 http://www.worldpolicy.org/sites/default/files/Dangerous%20Speech%20Guidelines%20 Benesch%20January%202012.pdf

Benesch, S. 2012. Words as Weapons, World Policy Journal, Vol. 29, no. 1, pp. 7–12.

Bleich, E. 2013. Freedom of Expression versus Racist Hate Speech: Explaining Differences Between High Court Regulations in the USA and Europe, *Journal of Ethnic and Migration Studies*, pp.2-37.

Bowman-Grieve, L. 2009. Exploring 'Stormfront': A Virtual Community of the Radical Right, *Studies in Conflict & Terrorism*, no. 11, pp. 989–1007.

Buckels, E.E., Trapnell, P.D. & Paulhus, D.L., 2014. Trolls just want to have fun. *Personality and individual Differences*, Vol. 67, pp. 97–102.

Buyse, A., 2014. Words of Violence:" Fear Speech," or How Violent Conflict Escalation Relates to the Freedom of Expression. *Human Rights Quarterly*, Vol. 36, no. 4, pp.779–97.

Citron, K. D. and Norton, H. 2011. Intermediaries and hate speech: Fostering digital citizenship for our information age. *Boston University Law Review,* Vol. 91, pp. 1435–84.

Chang, J. et al., 2014. *The Causes and Consequences of Group Violence: From Bullies to Terrorists*, Lexington Books.

Cheeseman, N. 2008. The Kenyan Elections of 2007: An Introduction, *Journal of Eastern African Studies* 2, no. 2, pp. 166–84.

Chorley, M. and Camber, R. 2014. Anti-terror unit to push to remove hate video from YouTue as Cameron vows to drive out 'extremist poison'. http://www.dailymail.co.uk/news/article-2665335/Video-hate-STILL-YouTube-Online-site-failing-stop-terrorists.html

Cao, Q. Sirivianos, M. Yang, X. and Pregueiro, T. 2011. Aiding the detection of fake accounts in large scale social online services. https://www.usenix.org/system/files/conference/nsdi12/nsdi12-final42_2.pdf

Defeis, E.F., 1992. Freedom of speech and international norms: A response to hate speech. *Stan. Journal of International Law.*, Vol. 29, pp. 57–74.

De Koster, W. and Houtman, D. 2008. "'STORMFRONT IS LIKE A SECOND HOME TO ME' On Virtual Community Formation by Right-Wing Extremists," *Information, Communication & Society, Vol.* 11, no. 8, pp. 1169–85.

Duggan, M. 2014. Online Harassment: Summary of findings. http://www.pewinternet.org/2014/10/22/online-harassment/

Epstein, K. 2014. "Twitter teams up with advocacy group to fight online harassment of women". http://www.theguardian.com/technology/2014/nov/08/twitter-harassment-women-wam

Foxman, A.H. & Wolf, C., 2013. *Viral hate: Containing its spread on the Internet*. Macmillan.

Erjavec, K. & Kovačič, M.P., 2012. "You Don't Understand, This is a New War!" Analysis of Hate Speech in News Web Sites' Comments. *Mass Communication and Society*, Vol. 15, no. 6, pp.899–920.

Herman, B. 2014. "WAM! And Twitter tackle problem of online harassment of women". http://www.ibtimes. com/wam-twitter-tackle-problem-online-harassment-women-1720876

Hindstrom, H. 2012. "State Media Issues Correction after Publishing Racial Slur," *DVB Multimedia Group*, June 6, 2012, https://www.dvb.no/news/state-media-issues-correction-after-publishing-racial-slur/22328

Hoechsmann, M. and Poyntz, S. R. 2012. *Media Literacies. A Critical Introduction.* Oxford: Wiley-Blackwell.

Holland, H. 2014. "Facebook in Myanmar: Amplifying Hate Speech?," June 14, 2014, http://www. aljazeera.com/indepth/features/2014/06/facebook-myanmar-rohingya-amplifying-hate-speech-2014612112834290144.html

Ghanea, N., 2008. Article 19 and 20 of the ICCPR. In Expert Seminar on the Links between Articles 19 and 20 of the ICCPR. Geneva.

Ghanea, N., 2013. Intersectionality and the Spectrum of Racist Hate Speech: Proposals to the UN Committee on the Elimination of Racial Discrimination. *Human Rights Quarterly*, Vol. 35, no. 4, pp.935–54.

Goldsmith, J.L. & Wu, T., 2006. Who controls the Internet? Illusions of a borderless world, Oxford University Press New York. http://jost.syr.edu/wp-content/uploads/who-controls-the-internet_illusions-of-a-borderless-world.pdf

Goodman, E and Cherubini, F. 2013. *Online comment moderation: emerging best practices. A guide to promoting robust and civil online conversation.* http://www.wan-ifra.org/reports/2013/10/04/online-comment-moderation-emerging-best-practices

Herring, S. et al., 2002. Searching for safety online: Managing"trolling" in a feminist forum. *The Information Society*, Vol. 18, no. 5, pp.371–84.

Hoechsmann, M. and Poyntz, S. R. 2012. *Media Literacies. A Critical Introduction.* Oxford: Wiley-Blackwell.

Howell, J. and Lind, J. 2009. *Counter-Terrorism, Aid and Civil Society: Before and after the War on Terror.* New York: Palgrave-Macmillan, 2009.

HRC. 2015. *Report of the Special Rapporteur on minority issues, Rita Izsák.* A/HRC/28/64

In Other Words Project. 2013. *Toolbox.* Available online at: http://www.inotherwords-project.eu/sites/default/files/Toolbox.pdf

iHub Research. 2013. *Umati Final Report.* http://www.research.ihub.co.ke/uploads/2013/june/1372415606__936.pdf

Kanyinga, K. 2009. The Legacy of the White Highlands: Land Rights, Ethnicity and the Post-2007 Election Violence in Kenya, *Journal of Contemporary African Studies, Vol.* 27, no. 3, pp. 325–44.

Kelion, L. 2013. *Facebook lets beheading clips return to social network.* http://www.bbc.co.uk/news/technology-24608499 (Accessed 15 December 2014.)

Kellow, C.L. & Steeves, H.L., 1998. The role of radio in the Rwandan genocide. *Journal of Communication*, Vol. 48, no. 3, pp.107–28.

Kiersons, S. 2013. "The Colonial Origins of Hate Speech in Burma," October 28, 2013, https://thesentinelproject. org/2013/10/28/the-colonial-origins-of-hate-speech-in-burma/

Kinetz, E. 2013. "New Numerology of Hate Grows in Burma," April 29, 2013, http://www.irrawaddy.org/religion/new-numerology-of-hate-grows-in-burma.html

Kohl, U., 2002. Eggs, Jurisdiction, and the Internet. *International and comparative law quarterly*, Vol. 51, no. 3, pp.556–582.

Laclau, E. and Mouffe, C. 1985. *Hegemony and Socialist Strategy. Towards a Radical Democratic Politics.* London: Verso, 1985.

Leo, L.A., Gaer, F.D. & Cassidy, E.K., 2011. Protecting Religions from Defamation: A Threat to Universal Human Rights Standards. *Harv. JL & Pub. Pol'y*, Vol. 34, pp.769–95.

MacKinnon, R. et al., 2015. Fostering Freedom Online: The Role of Internet Intermediaries, Paris: UNESCO.

Mamdani, M. 2010. *Saviors and Survivors: Darfur, Politics, and the War on Terror.* Random House LLC.

Meddaugh, P. M. and Kay, J. 2009. Hate Speech or 'Reasonable Racism?' The Other in Stormfront, *Journal of Mass Media Ethics, Vol.* 24, no. 4, pp. 251–68.MediaSmarts .NDa.

MediaSmarts. Facing online hate. Available online at: http://mediasmarts.ca/tutorial/facing-online-hate-tutorial

MediaSmarts. *NDb Awards and recognitions*. Available at: http://mediasmarts.ca/about-us/awards-recognitions

Morsink, J., 1999. *The universal declaration of human rights: Origins, drafting, and intent*. University of Pennsylvania Press.

2012. "Contents removed from racist Facebook page". Available online, at: http://www.smh.com.au/technology/technology-news/contents-removed-from-racist-facebook--page-20120808-23tr1.html

Mossberger, K. Tolbert, C. J. and Mcneal, R. S. 2008. *Digital Citizenship. The Internet, Society and Participation.* London: The MIT Press, 2008.

No Hate Speech Movement'. 2013a. Campaign tools and materials. Available online at: http://nohate.ext.coe.int/Campaign-Tools-and-Materials

No Hate Speech Movement. 2013b. No Hate Ninja Project - A Story About Cats, Unicorns and Hate Speech. Available online at: https://www.youtube.com/watch?v=kp7ww3KvccE

No Hate Speech Movement. 2014. Follow-Up Group, Fifth Meeting. Available online at: http://nohate.ext.coe.int/The-Campaign/Follow-Up-Group-of-the-Joint-Council-on-Youth2

Nowak, M., 1993. *UN covenant on civil and political rights: CCPR commentary*. NP Engel Kehl.

Oboler, A. 2012. An Online Hate Prevention Institute report on Aboriginal Memes and Online Hate. http://ohpi.org.au/reports/IR12-2-Aboriginal-Memes.pdf

Online Hate Prevention Institute. 2014. "Press release: Launch of online tool to combat hate". http://ohpi.org.au/press-release-launch-of-online-tool-to-combat-hate/

Osborn, M. 2008. Fuelling the Flames: Rumour and Politics in Kibera, *Journal of Eastern African Studies, Vol.* 2, no. 2, pp. 315–27.

Osler, A. and Starkey, H. 2005. *Changing Citizenship.* Berkshire: Open University Press.

Peterson, A. and Knowles, C. 2009. "Active Citizenship: A Preliminary Study into Student Teacher Understandings," *Educational Research* 51, no. 1 (March 2009): 39–59, doi:10.1080/00131880802704731.

Post, R., Hare, I. & Weinstein, J., 2009. Hate speech. In *Extreme speech and democracy*, Oxford University Press, pp.123–38.

Ribble, M. 2011. *Digital Citizenship in Schools: Nine Elements All Students Should Know.* ISTE, 2011.

Rosen, *The harm in hate speech*, Harvard University Press.

Rosenfeld, M., 2012. Hate Speech in Constitutional Jurisprudence. In *The Content and Context of Hate Speech*, Cambridge University Press, pp. 242-89.

Rowbottom, J., 2012. To Rant, Vent and Converse: Protecting Low Level Digital Speech. *The Cambridge Law Journal*, Vol, 71, n.2, pp.355–383.

Ryngaert, C., 2008. *Jurisdiction in international law*. Oxford University Press.

Schissler, M. 2014a. "Echo Chambers in Myanmar: Social Media and the Ideological Justifications for Mass Violence" (presented at the Communal Conflict in Myanmar: Characteristics, Causes, Consequences, Yangon, 2014). Causes, Consequences, Yangon, 2014

Schissler, M. 2014b. "May Flowers," *New Mandala*, May 17, 2014, http://asiapacific.anu.edu.au/newmandala/2014/05/17/may-flowers/

Schomerus, M., Allen, T. and Vlassenroot, K. 2012. KONY 2012 and the Prospects for Change, *Foreign Affairs*.

Shin, J., 2008. Morality and Internet Behavior: A study of the Internet Troll and its relation with morality on the Internet. In Society for Information Technology & Teacher Education International Conference. pp. 2834–40.

Somerville, K. 2011. Violence, Hate Speech and Inflammatory Broadcasting in Kenya: The Problems of Definition and Identification, *Ecquid Novi: African Journalism Studies, Vol.* 32, no. 1, pp. 82–101.

Stremlau, N., 2011. The press and the political restructuring of Ethiopia. *Journal of Eastern African Studies*, Vol. 5, no. 4, pp.716–32.

Stremlau, N., 2012. Somalia: Media law in the absence of a state. *International Journal of Media & Cultural Politics*, Vol. 8, no. 2-3, pp.159–74.

Tan, M. 2014. "Myanmar's First Non-Government Phone Carrier, Ooredoo, Goes Live," *CNET*, August 6, 2014, http://www.cnet.com/uk/news/myanmar-first-non-government-phone-carrier-ooredoo-goes-live/

Tsesis, A., 2001. Hate in cyberspace: Regulating hate speech on the Internet. *San Diego L. Rev.*, Vol. 38, pp. 817-54.

Thompson, A., 2007. *The media and the Rwanda genocide*. IDRC.

Viljoen, F., 2012. *International human rights law in Africa.* Oxford University Press.

Waldron, J., 2012. *The harm in hate speech*. Harvard University Press.

Romano, A. 2013. "What will it take for Facebook to care about violence against women?" http://www.dailydot.com/business/wam-fbrape-violence-against-women-facebook/ (Accessed 22 December 2014.)

Yanagizawa-Drott, D., 2010. Propaganda and conflict: Theory and evidence from the Rwandan genocide. Working Paper, Harvard University.

Zhang, C. Sun, J. Zhu, X, and Fang, Y. 2010. Privacy and security for online social networks: Challenges and opportunities. *IEEE Network,* July/August Issue.

Notes

1   http://www.unesco.org/new/en/internetstudy

2   See Council of Europe, "Mapping study on projects against hate speech online", 15 April 2012. See also interviews: Christine Chen, Senior Manager for Public Policy, Google, 2 March 2015; Monika Bickert, Head of Global Policy Management, Facebook, 14 January 2015.

3   See HateBase – Hate speech statistics, http://www.hatebase.org/popular

4   Interview: Andre Oboler, CEO, Online Hate Prevention Institute, 31 October 2014.

5   See Chapter 4, Section 1 for more details.

6   There are cases of individuals who had to serve jail sentences for tweets written when drunk or for having jokingly tweeted they were planning to blowing up an airport (Rowbottom 2012).

7   Interview: Drew Boyd, Director of Operations, The Sentinel Project for Genocide Prevention, 24 October 2014.

8   Interview: Drew Boyd, Director of Operations, The Sentinel Project for Genocide Prevention, 24 October 2014.

10   This is a point also made by the UN Human Rights Council Special Rapporteur on Minority Issues (HRC, 2015)

11   UDHR, Art 7.

12   UDHR, Art 19.

13   Annotations on the text of the draft International Covenants on Human Rights, A/2929, 1 July 1955, para. 189.

14   Australia, New Zealand, the United Kingdom and the United States. See also Gelber, Katharine. Australia's Response to Articles 19 and 20 of the ICCPR. 2011 Expert Workshops on the Prohibition of Incitement to National, Racial or Religious Hatred, Bangkok, 6-7 July 2011, p. 3.

15   Human Rights Committee. General Comment no. 11, Article 20: Prohibition of Propaganda for War and Inciting National, Racial or Religious Hatred, 29 July 1983, para. 2. In 2011, The Committee elucidated its views on the relationship of Article 19 and 20 when it reaffirmed that the provisions complement each other and that Article 20 "may be considered as *lex specialis* with regard to Article 19". Human Rights Committee. General Comment no. 34, Article 19: Freedoms of opinion and expression, CCPR/C/GC/34, 12 September 2011, paras. 48-52.

16   Article 19 (2) of the ICCPR, italics added.

17   It is worthy to mention that the expression "of all kinds" was reproduced in the Article 13 (1) of the American Convention on Human Rights, but not in the European Convention on Human Rights or the African Charter on Human Rights and Peoples' Rights.

18   Article 19 (2) of the ICCPR.

19   Human Rights Committee General Comment 34, *supra* note **Error! Bookmark not defined.**, para. 12.

20   *Ibid.*, para. 15.

21   Article 19 (3) if the ICCPR.

22   Article 5 (1) of the ICCPR.

23   Human Rights Council. Report of the Special Rapporteur on the Promotion and Protection of the Right to Freedom of Opinion and Expression, Frank La Rue, A/HRC/14/23, 20 April 2010, para. 77.

24   Human Rights Committee General Comment 34, *supra* note **Error! Bookmark not defined.**, para. 43

25   Even the Human Rights Committee, which has decided on cases concerning Article 20, has avoided providing a definition of incitement to hatred. Human Rights Council. Incitement to Racial and Religious Hatred and the Promotion of Tolerance: Report of the High Commissioner for Human Rights, A/HRC/2/6, 20 September 2006, para. 36.

26   Faurisson v. France , C. Individual opinion by Elizabeth Evatt and David Kretzmer, co-signed by Eckart Klein (concurring), para. 4.

27   Human Rights Council. Report of the United Nations High Commissioner for Human Rights Addendum, Expert seminar on the links between articles 19 and 20 of the International Covenant on Civil and Political Rights, A/HRC/10/31/Add.3, 16 January 2009, para. 1.

28   Report of the High Commissioner for Human Rights, A/HRC/2/6, *supra* note 25, para. 73

29   "In Russia, for example, NGOs have regularly reported abuse of anti-extremist legislation, under which authorities have brought charges against religious groups [...] of incitement to hatred". Petrova, Dimitrina. Incitement to National, Racial or Religious Hatred: Role of Civil Society and National Human Rights Institutions. 2011 Expert Workshops on the Prohibition of Incitement to National, Racial or Religious Hatred, Vienna, 9-10 February 2011, para. 3.

30   *The Camden Principles*, para. 12 (3).

31   Conclusions and recommendations emanating from the four regional expert workshop organized by the OHCHR in 2011 and adopted by experts in Rabat, Morocco on 5 October 2012, available at: http://www.ohchr.org/Documents/Issues/Opinion/SeminarRabat/Rabat_draft_outcome.pdf

32   Conclusions and recommendations emanating from the four regional expert workshop organized by the OHCHR in 2011 and adopted by experts in Rabat, Morocco on 5 October 2012, available at: http://www.ohchr.org/Documents/Issues/Opinion/SeminarRabat/Rabat_draft_outcome.pdf

33   Ibid.

34   Report of the High Commissioner for Human Rights, A/HRC/2/6, para. 39;

35   Committee on the Elimination of Racial Discrimination, General Recommendation 29, Discrimination Based on Descent (Sixty-first session, 2002), U.N. Doc. A/57/18 at 111 (2002), reprinted in Compilation of General Comments and General Recommendations Adopted by Human Rights Treaty Bodies, U.N. Doc. HRI\GEN\1\Rev.6 at 223 (2003), paras. r, s and t

36   Article 2 of the CEDAW.

37   General recommendation No. 28 on the core obligations of States parties under article 2 of the Convention on the Elimination of All Forms of Discrimination against Women Para. 19

38   HRC Resolution 17/19, Human rights, sexual orientation and gender identity, A/HRC/RES/17/19, 14 July 2011, preambular part.

39   Human Rights Committee, General Comment 28, Equality of rights between men and women (article 3), U.N. Doc. CCPR/C/21/Rev.1/Add.10 (2000), para 22.

40   Article 13 (4) of the American Convention on Human Rights.

41   Inter-American Commission on Human Rights. Inter-American Declaration of Principles on Freedom of Expression, 20 October 2000, para. 7.

42   Inter-American Commission on Human Rights, Advisory Opinion OC-5/85, 13 November 1985, para. 39

43   Ibid., para 39.

44   Ibid., para 39.

45   African Commission on Human and Peoples' Rights. Declaration of Principles on Freedom of Expression in Africa, 32nd Session, Banjul, 17 - 23 October 2002.

46   Organization of the Islamic Conference, Cairo Declaration on Human Rights in Islam, preambular section, 5 August 1990.

47   Organization of Islamic Cooperation, Sixth OIC Observatory Report on Islamophobia, Presented to the 40th Council of Foreign Ministers, Conakry, Republic of Guinea, December 2013, p 31.

48   Article 22 of the CDHRI.

49   League of Arab States, Arab Charter on Human Rights, 22 May, 2004, entered into force 15 March 2008, para. 32 (1)

50   *Ibid.*, para. 32 (2).

51   Human Rights Committee, General Comment 22, Article 18 (Forty-eighth session, 1993). Compilation of General Comments and General Recommendations Adopted by Human Rights Treaty Bodies, U.N. Doc. HRI/GEN/1/Rev.1 at 35 (1994).

52   Article 7 of the ASEAN Human Rights Declaration.

53   United Nations Office of the High Commissioner for Human Rights, 'ASEAN Human Rights Declaration Should Maintain International Standards', An Open Letter from the Coordination Committee of the Special Procedures of the Human Rights Council on the draft ASEAN Human Rights Declaration, 1 November 2012.

54   Article 54 of the Charter of Fundamental Rights of the European Union.

55   Article 10 of the European Convention on Human Rights.

56   Handyside v. the United Kingdom, 7 December 1976, para. 49. More cases of hate Speech under the European Court can be found at: http://www.echr.coe.int/Documents/FS_Hate_speech_ENG.pdf 49

57   ECRI General Policy Recommendation No. 6, On Combating the Dissemination of Racist, Xenophobic and Antisemitic Material via the Internet, adopted on 15 December 2000.

58   Council of Europe, *Convention on Cybercrime*, 23 November 2001, paras 31-34.

59   Council of Europe, *Additional Protocol to the Convention on cybercrime, concerning the criminalisation of acts of a racist and xenophobic nature committed through computer systems*, 28 January 2003, art 5 para 1.

60   Article 19 (3), subparagraphs (a) and (b), of the ICCPR. (italics added).

61   Human Rights Committee General Comment 34, *supra* note 19, para. 22.

62   Rabat Plan of Action, para 14.

63   Human Rights Committee General Comment 34, *supra* para. **Error! Bookmark not defined.**.

64   http://www.ohchr.org/Documents/Publications/GuidingPrinciplesBusinessHR_EN.pdf,Principle 11.

65   http://www.ohchr.org/Documents/Publications/GuidingPrinciplesBusinessHR_EN.pdf, principle 17.

66   http://www.ohchr.org/Documents/Publications/GuidingPrinciplesBusinessHR_EN.pdf, principle 22.

67   Natasha Lomas, #Gamergate Shows Tech Needs Far Better Algorithms, Techcrunch, 18 October 2014. http://techcrunch.com/2014/10/18/gamergate-tactics/

68   In March 2015, for example, Facebook updated its community guidelines to provide greater clarity on specific types of content that it moderates, including messages from organizations considered "dangerous". See Leo Kelion, "Facebook revamps its takedown guidelines", BBC, 16 March 2015, http://m.bbc.co.uk/news/technology-31890521

69   http://help.yahoo.com/l/us/yahoo/smallbusiness/bizmail/spam/spam-44.html

70   https://twitter.com/tos

71   https://support.twitter.com/entries/18311

72   https://www.youtube.com/t/community_guidelines

73   https://www.facebook.com/communitystandards

74   https://www.facebook.com/communitystandards

75   http://msdn.microsoft.com/en-us/library/windows/apps/hh184842(v=vs.105).aspx

76   http://www.xbox.com/en-GB/legal/codeofconduct

77   Robert Glancy, "Will you read this article about terms and conditions? You really should do", The Guardian, 24 April 2014. http://www.theguardian.com/commentisfree/2014/apr/24/terms-and-conditions-online-small-print-information

78   One of these initiatives is "Terms of Service. Didn't Read", which rates the ToS of some of the most important internet intermediaries and applications. The initiative can be accessed at https://tosdr.org.

79   See LICRA et UEJF v. Yahoo! Inc. et Yahoo Fr., T.G.I. Paris, 22 May 2000; See also Ministerio Publico Federal v. Google Brasil Internet Ltda, 17a Vara Cível São Paulo, Proc. No. 2006.61.00.018332-8 30 August 2006.

80   Guy Berger, "Barbarians and gatekeepers" Presentation to: International Symposium on Freedom of Expression, UNESCO, Paris, 26 January 2011. http://www.unesco.org/new/fileadmin/MULTIMEDIA/HQ/CI/CI/pdf/Events/International_Symposium_on_Freedom_of_Expression/presentations/guy_berger_symposium_foe_26_january.pdf. See also Lwanga Mwilu, "Framing the foreigner : a close reading of readers' comments on Thought leader blogs on xenophobia published between May and June", 2008. http://contentpro.seals.ac.za/iii/cpro/DigitalItemViewPage.external?sp=1002927

81   Adrian Chen, "Inside Facebook's outsourced anti-porn and gore brigade, where 'camel toes' are more offensive then 'crushed heads'", Gawker, 16 February 2012, http://gawker.com/5885714/inside-facebooks-outsourced-anti-porn-and-gore-brigade-where-camel-toes-are-more-offensive-than-crushed-heads.

82   Jeffrey Rosen, http://www.newrepublic.com/article/113045/free-speech-Internet-silicon-valley-making-rules

83   Interview: Monika Bickert, Head of Global Policy Management, Facebook, 14 January 2015.

84   Josh Constine, "Track Your Facebook Abuse, Bullying, Spam Reports With Transparent New Support Dashboard", TechCrunch, 26 April 2012. http://techcrunch.com/2012/04/26/facebook-support-dashboard

85   Shiv Malik, Sandra Laville, Elena Cresci and Aisha Gani, "Isis in duel with Twitter and YouTube to spread extremist propaganda", The Guardian, 24 September 2014. http://www.theguardian.com/world/2014/sep/24/isis-twitter-youtube-message-social-media-jihadi

86   "Google removes Singapore hate-speech blog targeting Filipinos", The Malay Mail Online, 20 June 2014. http://www.themalaymailonline.com/tech-gadgets/article/google-removes-singapore-hate-speech-blog-targeting-filipinos

87   Doug Gross, "Twitter faces new pressure to limit hate speech", CNN, 31 July 2013. www.cnn.
      com/2013/07/30/tech/social-media/twitter-hate-speech

88   Kim Graham, "Petition: Add A Report Abuse Button To Tweets", Change.org, http://www.change.org/p/
      twitter-add-a-report-abuse-button-to-tweets

89   Humanitarian Policy Group, "Crisis in Kenya: land, displacement and the search for 'durable solutions'",
      12 April 2008.

90   Interview: Nanjira Sambuli, Project Lead, UMATI, 26 November 2014.

91   Hereward Holland, "Facebook in Myanmar: Amplifying Hate Speech?," Al Jazeera, 14 June 2014,
      http://www.aljazeera.com/indepth/features/2014/06/facebook-myanmar-rohingya-amplifying-hate-
      speech-2014612112834290144.html

92   "Why Is There Communal Violence in Myanmar?", BBC, 3 July 2014. http://www.bbc.co.uk/news/world-
      asia-18395788

93   Michael Tan, "Myanmar's First Non-Government Phone Carrier, Ooredoo, Goes Live," *CNET*, 6 August
      2014, http://www.cnet.com/uk/news/myanmar-first-non-government-phone-carrier-ooredoo-goes-live/

94   "Why Is There Communal Violence in Myanmar?", BBC, 3 July 2014. http://www.bbc.co.uk/news/world-
      asia-18395788

95   Andrew Marshall, "Special Report: Plight of Muslim Minority Threatens Myanmar Spring," Reuters, 15 June
      2012, http://www.reuters.com/article/2012/06/15/us-myanmar-rohingya-idUSBRE85E06A20120615

96   Erika Kinetz, "New Numerology of Hate Grows in Burma", Irrawaddy, 29 April 2013 http://www.irrawaddy.
      org/religion/new-numerology-of-hate-grows-in-burma.html. Hereward Holland, "Facebook in Myanmar:
      Amplifying Hate Speech?," Al Jazeera, 14 June 2014; Steven Kiersons, "The Colonial Origins of Hate
      Speech in Burma", The Sentinel Project, 28 October 2013, https://thesentinelproject.org/2013/10/28/
      the-colonial-origins-of-hate-speech-in-burma/., http://www.aljazeera.com/indepth/features/2014/06/
      facebook-myanmar-rohingya-amplifying-hate-speech-2014612112834290144.html

97   Tim McLaughlin, "Facebook takes steps to combat hate speech", The Myanmar Times, 25 July 2014.
      http://www.mmtimes.com/index.php/national-news/11114-facebook-standards-marked-for-translation.
      html

98   Ibrahim Sah, "Burma, US pledge to fight hate speech", The Burma Times, 4 October 2014. http://
      burmatimes.net/burma-us-pledge-to-fight-hate-speech.

99   San Yamin Aung, "Burmese Online Activist Discusses Campaign Against Hate Speech", Irrawaddy, http://
      www.irrawaddy.org/interview/hate-speech-pours-poison-heart.html

100   Interview: Myat Ko Ko, Justice Base, 24 November 2014.

101   Interview: Harry Myo Lin, Panzagar, 12 December 2014.

102   Interview: Christopher Wolf, ADL, 13 November 2014.

103   Interview: Drew Boyd, Director of Operations, the Sentinel Project for Genocide Prevention, 24 October
      2014.

104   Interview: Drew Boyd, Director of Operations, the Sentinel Project for Genocide Prevention, 24 October
      2014.

105   Interview: Andre Oboler, CEO, Online Hate Prevention Institute, 31 October 2014.

106   Interview: Imran Awan, Birmingham City University, 21 November 2014.

107   Tell Mama. 2014. For more information please see: http://tellmamauk.org

108 Facebook. 2013. "Controversial, harmful and hateful, speech on Facebook". https://www.facebook.com/notes/facebook-safety/controversial-harmful-and-hateful-speech-on-facebook/574430655911054

109 BBC. 2012. "Facebook removes 'racist' page in Australia". http://www.bbc.co.uk/news/world-asia-19191595

110 Toor, A. 2012. "Facebook faces hate speech criticism over 'Aboriginal memes' page". http://www.theverge.com/2012/8/8/3227329/facebook-hate-speech-aborigine-memes-australia

111 Jacinta O'Keefe. 2012. "Petition: Immediately remove the racist page called 'Aboriginal Memes'" Change.org. https://www.change.org/p/facebook-headquarters-immediately-remove-the-racist-page-called-aboriginal-memes

112 Interview: Andre Oboler, CEO, Online Hate Prevention Institute, 31 October 2014.

113 More information about the Women, Action and the Media group is available on their official website, at: http://www.womenactionmedia.org/why-wam/what-we-do/

114 More information about the Everyday Sexism project is available on their official website, at: http://www.everydaysexism.com/index.php/about

115 For a list of the fifteen companies please see: WAM! (2013). *Campaign wins and updates: It worked!* Available online, at: http://www.womenactionmedia.org/facebookaction/campaign-wins-updates/

116 John Raines. 2013. "Petition: Demand Facebook remove pages that promote sexual violence". Change.org. https://www.change.org/p/demand-facebook-remove-pages-that-promote-sexual-violence

117 Garossino, S. 2013. "How Facebook learned rape is bad for business". http://www.huffingtonpost.ca/sandy-garossino/wam-facebooks-pr-disaster_b_3357187.html

118 Facebook. 2013. "Controversial, harmful and hateful, speech on Facebook", International Business Times, 7 November 2014, https://www.facebook.com/notes/facebook-safety/controversial-harmful-and-hateful-speech-on-facebook/574430655911054

119 Ibid.

120 Barbara Herman, "WAM! And Twitter tackle problem of online harassment of women". http://www.ibtimes.com/wam-twitter-tackle-problem-online-harassment-women-1720876

121 Arce, N. 2014. "Twitter, WAM! partnership now makes it possible to report gender-based harassment on Twitter". http://www.techtimes.com/articles/19692/20141107/twitter-wam-partnership-now-makes-it-possible-to-report-gender-based-harassment-on-twitter.htm

122 Kayla Epstein, "Twitter teams up with advocacy group to fight online harassment of women", The Guardian, 10 November 2014 http://www.theguardian.com/technology/2014/nov/08/twitter-harassment-women-wam

123 WAM!, "To combat the harassment of women online, Women, Action and the Media (WAM!) announce a new partnership with Twitter". http://www.womenactionmedia.org/cms/assets/uploads/2014/11/Twitterprojectpressrelease-1.pdf

124 WAM!, "WAM Twitter harassment reporting tool". https://womenactionmedia.wufoo.com/forms/ztaetji1jrhv10/

125 Interview: Monika Bickert and Ciara Lyden, Global Policy Management, Facebook, 14 January 2015.

126 Twitter, *We hear you.* https://blog.twitter.com/en-gb/2013/we-hear-you

127 Kim Graham, "Petition: Add A Report Abuse Button To Tweets", Change.org, http://www.change.org/p/twitter-add-a-report-abuse-button-to-tweets

128 Google, "Transparency Report". http://www.google.com/transparencyreport/

129 http://www.unesco.org/new/en/global-citizenship-education

130 Paris Declaration on MIL in the Digital Era. http://www.unesco.org/new/en/communication-and-information/resources/news-and-in-focus-articles/in-focus-articles/2014/paris-declaration-on-media-and-information-literacy-adopted/

131 The 'No Hate Speech Movement' is a regional campaign that encompasses 50 countries far beyond the European Continent. Although the campaign has common goals and develops joint strategies, the particular projects and initiatives rune in every country are the responsibility of the National coordinators and subject to the capacity and resources in each country.

132 Interview: Laura Geraghty, No Hate Speech Movement, 25 November 2014.

133 Media Smarts, "Young Canadians in a wired world. Teachers' perspectives", 2012.

134 Interview: Matthew Johnson, Director of Education, Media Smarts, 15 November 2014.

135 No Hate Speech Movement, Campaign tools and materials. Available online at: http://nohate.ext.coe.int/Campaign-Tools-and-Materials

136 No Hate Speech Movement, No Hate Ninja Project - A Story About Cats, Unicorns and Hate Speech. Available online at: https://www.youtube.com/watch?v=kp7ww3KvccE

137 MediaSmarts, Facing online hate. Available online at: http://mediasmarts.ca/tutorial/facing-online-hate-tutorial

138 In Other Words Project, Toolbox. Available online at: http://www.inotherwords-project.eu/sites/default/files/Toolbox.pdf

139 Aileen Donegan, "Debate 2: 'Hate speech is more than free speech'", No HAte Speech Movement Forum, 17 October 2013, http://forum.nohatespeechmovement.org/discussion/6/debate-2-hate-speech-is-more-than-free-speech/p1

140 No Hate Speech Movement, Follow-Up Group, Fifth Meeting. Available online at: http://nohate.ext.coe.int/The-Campaign/Follow-Up-Group-of-the-Joint-Council-on-Youth2

141 https://en-gb.facebook.com/help/128548343894719

142 Article 19. Internet Intermediaries: Dilemma of Liability Q and A. http://www.article19.org/resources.php/resource/37243/en/internet-intermediaries:-dilemma-of-liability-q-and-a

143 See for example the study of Stormfront by De Koster and Houtman (2008) mentioned in Chapter 5.

144 See for example the article by Rowbottom (2012) and the "Jane Austin Row" mentioned in Chapter 4.

145 See Susan Benesch, 2014. Troll Wrastling for Beginners: Data-Driven Methods to Decrease Hatred Online, http://cyber.law.harvard.edu/events/luncheon/2014/03/benesch; and Ethan Zuckerman, 2014. Susan Benesch on dangerous speech and counterspeech, http://www.ethanzuckerman.com/blog/2014/03/25/susan-benesch-on-dangerous-speech-and-counterspeech/